THE SLAVES HAVE NAMES

ANCESTORS OF MY HOME

ANDI CUMBO-FLOYD

Printed in the United States of America

First Printing 2013

Cover Design by Stephanie Spino—Stephaniespino.com

Proofreading by Ranee Tomlin - wordsforstories.com

The Slaves Have Names / ISBN 9781733771320

❀ Created with Vellum

For the people who were enslaved at Bremo.
You built the place I call my home with the sweat of your brow and the
bent of your back. I hope I have done you just the smallest amount of
justice.

1

THE SLAVE CEMETERY

The graveyard sits in a copse of trees surrounded by a deteriorating stone wall. Most who know these farms well know it's there, but I don't think anyone really visits except me. My favorite person from this plantation is buried here. His name is Primus, and I think he can hear me.

In the late afternoons sometimes, I walk up and talk to the folks who are buried in the undulating earth. Most of their graves are unmarked by any stone except, perhaps, two pieces of slate stuck vertically in the ground, one at head and one at foot, and long worn down or washed clean of names. But three stones bear words, gifts cut into rock—Ben Creasy, the carpenter; Jesse Nicholas, the stonemason; and Primus, the foreman.

Ben's and Jesse's stones are clear—with their names and dates marked deeply in the sandstone. I can find them in the records— know for sure who they are.

Primus's stone is harder to know. The tradition here on the farm is that Primus, the foreman at Upper Bremo, is buried here, but I cannot be sure. The stone reads, "Prams—12," and I'm not sure that refers to this Primus. It may be his grandson, also Primus, or some person I don't know yet. It's the 12 that throws me—my Primus lived to be an old man, long past 1812; his death date is noted: 1849. That date seems right according to the records, but then, the records are so sparse, it's hard to know. I don't know how to solidify—to give storied flesh—to these rough marks hewn deep into stone.

Still, I expect my Primus is buried here, somewhere, and it's to him that I speak. On days when the world just doesn't make sense, I tell him the tangles . . . and in the breathing air of that cemetery, I feel the strands loosen, as if Primus has taken them in his strong, wide fingers and untwisted them.

In that cemetery, at least 100 people are buried. Their graves unmarked, their stories untold. Their lives left twisted-together strands: a note about a doctor's visit, a listing on an inventory, a mention in a diary or letter. Primus cannot stretch out their stories. Though, I expect him to. He is the patriarch of this place to me. The man I see carrying the stories. Yet, I cannot hear him speak them.

In these gravestones, it is the absence of rock that reveals, what has been carved away that speaks. Some days it feels as if I am making stories from the finest dust. Holy, frustrating, heart-breaking work.

ONE WINTER MORNING, I was walking the grounds of this place, up the road from the graveyard, deep in the grief of my mother's death a month past. The frost was heavy, and as I came around the corner by the biggest house here, I saw the last standing mulberry tree, the final remnant of the original owner's quick money plan for raising silkworms. The tree is long since healthy, now just a craggy trunk with a few branches spread thin and wide, like the last, wide-spaced breaths of life.

But this morning, the frost had glittered the spiderwebs that hung in these branches, ornaments created, it seemed, for me.

On this same path a few weeks before, Someone had whispered for just my ears, "Write about the slaves." I stopped my stride. Tears pricked my eyes. I knew this to be a request, a suggestion, a marker for the next steps of this life journey. Gifts hang in the air.

So I began, I began with the stories I knew . . . the few stories of Primus and Cato, whose names had survived in the owner's family stories for reasons no one knew. The letters collected from slaves emancipated to Liberia. The stories local historians could tell me. The 195 boxes tucked into acid-free folders inside archival crates in climate-controlled rooms at the University of Virginia. And I began to craft my own ornaments, tiny stories to hang on the tree that is this place.

Now, as I pass that mulberry, I see these stories, the tales slaves whispered to themselves as they passed that same tree, then ripe with green. The narratives written in the journals the master here kept. The anecdotes told in the stables as slave postilions prepared the horses to be hitched up. The legends repeated as the rare group of visitors sees this place now, the same as it ever was . . . almost.

The tree is filling out with ornaments, mostly unnoticed except in the right light by eyes that are ready and willing. The stories I most want told.

Sometime in college—when my world swung wider and I saw oppression in the lectures and slides of classes—it occurred to me that I had never heard talk of the people who built these plantations that I call home. Silence surrounded these enslaved people.

As I thought deeper into this silence, I came to imagine— wrongly, I now know—that the people I rode the bus with most days in high school—the black people who filled every seat but those held by my brother and me—may have been descended from the people who built the buildings and cleared the land that now gave my family its livelihood.

I wanted those stories, to wrap them like beads around my wrist. I wanted to know these people because, it seemed, no one else knew them or cared to.

The silence around the lives of 246 men, women, and children finally screamed out to me in that whispered morning. It was time.

THIS, then, is the story of people, people nearly forgotten and unnamed in the history of this place. The story of slavery, the story of presence in absence and voice in silence. It is also my story, the story of how 246 enslaved people pulled me back to live when it seemed the death of my mother might silence me forever. I am indebted to them—246 people who barely make a note in our written history—for my life and for this book. To them, and to my mother, I say, "You will not be forgotten. YOU will not be forgotten."

2

HAUNTED HALLOWEEN

We were just kids. Teenagers. I can honestly say we didn't know any better. But maybe we should have.

It was Halloween night. I was 17 and throwing a party. My friends and I were going to sleep in the barn for the night—eat pizza, hang out—and just enjoy the certain creepiness that can come with a slave plantation on an average day but is especially heightened by hormones and Halloween.

We started the evening in the barn. Most of the guys went out to get pizza. All of the girls and one of the boyfriends stayed behind. We were hanging out in the barn when Leigh Ann and Amy noticed a sound like a baseball rolling across the floor. We could hear it but not see it, whatever it was.

We looked around for an animal moving in the shadows or a branch scraping against a window. Nothing. "It's something under the floor," someone said. "It's a skull rolling around under the floor." The hysteria was mounting.

For a few minutes, I thought maybe there was something moving around in a space between the floor and the ceiling below. But then I remembered that there were only the heart pine boards that formed the floor and the ceiling of the stable-turned-root-cellar below. I knew better than to think something could be rolling against the floor from underneath, but I was caught up in the thrill of it, a willing scaredy-cat.

We ran to one side of the room, and the sound continued to move, sliding back and forth beneath the floor, a small terror we could not name. Then back across the room we went. Ten or fifteen minutes of this, and we were so scared that tears were coming.

Then, it stopped. We waited, barely breathing, and it didn't return. Relief. Deep breaths and nervous giggles.

Just then, the guys returned with the pizza, and we told them about the skull, laughing it off even as our heartbeats slowed. They decided—out of bravery, machismo, or just some sense of curiosity—to go to the cellar and check things out. Nothing. Just the sheets of black plastic over the saplings waiting to be planted in the tree nursery outside. We sat down and slapped open the pizza boxes.

As we took our first bites, the tapping started. Loud against the barn door by the field. This was impossible—the door's threshold opened about 10 feet over the ground. Someone would have to be floating there to knock on it.

No more skulls. Now, we had vampires to contend with.

Chad walked quietly toward the door, perhaps heartened by the presence of more testosterone in the room, retreating a few steps for every 10 or so he gained. Eventually, he slammed it open with a flat palm . . . and screamed. I think he leapt the entire distance of the barn back to us.

"There's a man there. A man. With a pitchfork," he said, his breath coming in gasps.

I heard the word "man" and said, "Dad!" I went over to look down out the door. There he was, a shovel handle at door level, grinning.

He came in, laughed with us awhile, and went on home, his Halloween job done.

We were already amped up by the time we went to the slave graveyard later. I don't say that as an excuse, just an explanation.

Once our heartbeats slowed, we returned to our pizza and talked about the things that made up our teenage days—band competitions and track meets, teacher flaws. About 11:30, we piled into two cars and drove up the road, past my house and to the graveyard. This was a planned part of the night, something I had offered as enticement to my friends. Midnight in the slave cemetery. On Halloween.

Jay parked his 1970s BMW 2002, and I pulled the Toyota right up next to him, just outside the short, slate wall. We got out, leaving the doors of the cars open so that we could see by the interior lights.

I either didn't think to bring flashlights or purposely left them to heighten the spooky factor. It's mighty dark in the country, can't-see-your-hand-in-front-of-your-face dark when there's not a moon. Creepier on Halloween for sure.

All in a bunch, my friends crossed the 20 or so feet to the cemetery, stepped onto the disintegrating wall, and dispersed.

I lingered back by the cars. I'm not sure why I did that except that the graveyard was familiar to me. Nothing new. Just a place up the road from my house.

I have this recollection that Jay was on the other side of the cemetery, a space that then seemed like acres away but really was probably about 200 feet across from me. I heard him yell.

Then Jodi, just a few feet away, screamed. "Someone grabbed me." Her high-pitched voice reached me. I could hear the roaring crackle of leaves and breath as everyone swarmed back toward the light.

For a few moments, we stood there trying to figure out what happened. Someone accused Chad of playing a trick. Jodi thought maybe Jay grabbed her arm. Oddly, no one suggested that my dad and I had rigged up another scare. We never did figure out what exactly happened, but I can say it wasn't Dad or me.

Quickly, we loaded the cars and went back to the barn. People were shaken. Leigh Ann sat close to Jay and comforted him. Chad held Jodi. Everyone was scared, and I don't think most of us slept that night. They were frightened; I was puzzled.

I still am. I don't know what my friends felt, heard, or saw. Right now, I can't even remember what Jay said had made him shout. I know they were genuinely scared, but maybe it was just the fright of the evening, fed by Dad's antics earlier, the exaggeration so easily achieved on a dark night. Or maybe something (someone?) reached out to them. If I were Primus or Letty or Hannah, I might have resented the use of my final resting place as a Halloween gimmick and decided to have a little fun of my own. I don't know what I think of that idea. I'm not even sure what I think of ghosts. I won't discount them, though.

What I do know is that now—20 years later—I go to that grave-yard to find peace. I don't feel scared or nervous there. Some-times sad, sometimes just quiet as I walk across the wavy ground, where—as best I can tell—at least 100 people are buried. Sometimes I go there and cut away saplings, trying to make it look more like a place that is cared for—since I do care for it a great deal—and less like a place where kids go to play on Halloween.

I'm ashamed of my choice to take my friends there that night. Not deeply ashamed—I give myself the grace of youth in my memory—but saddened that I did not see this as a place where people were buried, people who did not have a choice about their burial location, people whose graves go, largely, unmarked and unclaimed. I'm sad that I didn't take my friends there to meet these people.

I wish I had taken them to Primus's stone and said, "This is where Primus lies." That we didn't walk over to Ben Creasy's headstone and say, "Ben was a carpenter. His great-great-great-great-great-grandchildren go to school with us." That we didn't kneel beside Jesse Nicholas's stone—the stone of a skilled mason—and say, "Jesse's mom was the nurse for The General's kids. She is the only enslaved person buried in the family cemetery. I wonder how he felt to know he wouldn't be buried near her."

I don't know what my friends would have said to those things . . . teenage-glazed "uh-huhs," I expect. We were just kids, so caught in the drama of our own stories that it was hard to hear the people we knew, much less people who had been dead 150 years.

Still, I'm sorry I didn't say those things then. But now, these are the stories I tell when I take people, like my friend Joe Creasy, to see the stones. "Ben was a carpenter. He was your great-great-great-great-grandfather."

Then, I walk away and whisper to Primus a while.

3

PRIMUS RANDALL

Foreman. Husband of Betty. Father of Frank, Toby, Gilbert, Cary, Nancy, Dinah, and Lydia. Born 1770. Died 1849.

I AM FAIRLY certain his gravestone sits close to the place where the slate wall around the cemetery has fallen and corroded with rains and years, where we park on the grass and walk into the graveyard. A solid stone, it's made of sandstone and sits upright in the ground, unbroken, not leaning. A little slanted at the top, as if it was repurposed when it didn't fit a slot in a wall.

This slave cemetery is on Lower Bremo plantation, the place where my family still lives, the place I think of as home even though we never have owned the land there. My family came to live on Lower Bremo when I was 14 because my father took a job as the manager of a new tree nursery being established there on the middle of three plantations all started by the same man and still owned by his descendants. These three farms—as most people call them—are in a rural part of Central Virginia, a land that looks very much as it did when enslaved people first arrived there to clear the land with axes in the early 18th century.

Primus—an enslaved man—was the foreman on Upper Bremo, the largest of the three plantations. As foreman, Primus's job was to ensure that all the enslaved people did their work. He didn't discipline them—that was the work of the overseer—but he managed them, making certain that the crops were harvested and the garden tended, the livestock moved, and that there were enough hands at every task. He also sounded the bell to start and end the workday. In modern times, we would think of him as "middle management." Except that he didn't get paid for his labor or have any choice whether or not to take it on.

Some call people in his position "slave drivers," since technically he was the person who "drove" the work on the farm, but I cannot bear to lay that word against him. The lashing connotation is too painful.

I wonder if it was an honor for him to be the foreman, a point of privilege, maybe the kind of privilege that brings derision, like the kid who is the teacher's pet in class. Maybe other enslaved people sneered at him, disliked him because he was perceived as kowtowing to privilege. Maybe they saw him as the "Uncle Tom" before Uncle Tom was Uncle Tom.

Somehow, though—and maybe this says more about my wishful imagination than it does about the man—I can only picture him as respected by his friends and family. I just think that he was one of those people who managed to be esteemed by all who knew him. I have no basis for this idea since all I really know of him comes from tax lists, blanket distribution records, and slave inventories, but still, it seems true to me, the way I know something of a person's spirit by the way they speak to children.

He stands by the corncribs that now—in my time—have the patina of age. Then, they still held the gold of the heart pine from which he had hewn them. So much were these his buildings that an overseer called them "Primus' corn cribs."

His brow is damp in the six o'clock sun of a warm February evening, a pewter mug of water in his hand, filled quickly from the horse's trough nearby. His back is straight, but the pinched corners of his eyes speak of hard work and aching body. He watches as everyone walks past on their way home from the fields, nods to some and looks each in the eye, an acknowledgment that girds them as they pace homeward, upright for the first time in hours, hands caked with the soil of the low grounds by the river and blistered from wooden handles. The fields are fully hoed, ready for manuring tomorrow. Primus wants them to know he knows what this work took of them.

He stands there until each of them passes. He has been with them on and off all day, his back bent over that wood handle, too, because he does not require that anyone do work he won't do. He has honor, even in this job that pits him between master and slave in that space between powerless and truly empowered.

He does what he is asked—reports to the overseer who is sick and doesn't work, who drinks too much and beats his wife. Master thinks Primus does this for him, the paternal owner of this wide farm "family." But Primus knows better. He does it for them, to save them from what is worse—to be sold away from their mothers and children, to be whipped by the overseer who won't, even as he tries, look Primus in the eye. He has perfected the role of the middleman: to do as he's told but to find a way to do so without betraying his people, his kin, his family, his community.

At night, he lies down next to Betty and smells the sheep she has tended all day and beneath that the fragrance of her, salty and sweet. He nuzzles into her neck to breathe in the scent of home. His seven children drape themselves over each other on the low burlap mattresses covering the floor, and before he sleeps, Primus bends to touch each of them—a kiss on the cheek, a weighted hand on the shoulder. This small reminder that he is their father, their hope. He will not fail them.

Or so my imagination tells me.

What I do know of him, as fact, is that he lived to be about 76 years old and died here on this farm. The first mention I have of Primus is on a Fluvanna County personal-property tax list for 1782. His name is there, sandwiched between Charity and Mam. He was here, in this place, before any of the Cockes—his owner's family—lived here. This was his home first. His name appears again in the inventory from 1791. On the 1801 inventory, he's listed again, and then sporadically, over the next 20 years, when the overseers mention the daily tasks of running an agricultural enterprise.

In 1820, he received a blanket, and in 1822, he and his family received 1 bushel, 1 peck, and 1 gallon of meal—worth just about five dollars in today's economy. When his family and many others moved to the New Quarter down by the barn and on the other side of the creek, they got a blanket, a double bedstead, and two beds.

His daughter Lydia and her husband, Peyton, emigrated to Liberia in 1837 as free people. Lydia and Peyton Skipwith gave birth to Matilda, who married Samuel Lomax. Matilda and Samuel then had two daughters, Eliza Adala and Lydia Ann, who grew up as free people in Liberia. In 1840, Primus was counted as part of a census of the "Slaves at Upper and Lower Bremo" and listed, with Cato, as one of two "Male Slaves upward of 55 years and under 100."

This is not enough to know. It does not tell the story of this man —it does not give him flesh. It does not carry his dignity. It is only inventory, not story.

But it is all I can tell. Perhaps I have missed some references in the University of Virginia collections. Maybe the owner regales Primus's praises in the pages of his journal that I have not yet read. Maybe. But probably not.

Sometimes I walk up to the slave cemetery and kneel by Primus's grave. I talk to him about this book and what I hope to find. I read him this chapter and listen to the breeze in the oaks overhead to see if he approves.

Then, I whisper, "I want to tell you, Mr. Randall, that you did it. You made it. You lasted. You endured. I want to tell you that your strength was worth it. They made it. Those children of yours, they made it. Because of you. You have a story, and it lives on."

4

BEN CREASY

Carpenter. Husband of Judy. Father of Solomon, Jeffrey, Anthony, Jack, Cyrus, Leander, and Archer. Born 1779. Died 1833.

Iт's hard to connect who I know him to be, the faceless man buried by the gravestone with the man I read about on all these horrible, practical lists. That man on the page is imaginary to me, more fact than person. Ben is real. His very molecules are part of this place. I breathe him.

Today, I walked over to where his body is buried, and I laid my hand on his stone. I called him "Buddy." I hope that wasn't disrespectful; I called my brother "Buddy" for years. Ben and I are not really buddies; of course, I know this. I don't feel his equal. I am indebted to him—for this place, for the stories, for his name—"Ben Creasy" carved with care and filigree into stone. His stone is tangible. I can touch it. Lay my hands against the granite and feel something gritty, life carved into the death marker. Not just these photocopied names on long pieces of paper that don't really fit in the short folders I own. I can put my fingers into the grooves of the 5 and the 4—aged 54. Younger than my own father is now.

I DON'T KNOW Ben's scent—the way his body smelled fresh from a wash in the stream or his precious saltiness after a day in the field. But I know the fragrance of the cologne his four-times great-grandson Joe, my friend Joseph Creasy, wears. The scent of sandalwood and smiles. At 70, Joe looks fewer than the 54 years Ben lived and drives his spotless red Cadillac like he's 16 and fresh out of the gate.

Joe and I met through mutual friends—genealogists who had researched Joe's family. They told me he would be very interested in my work since his ancestors had been enslaved here, and so I emailed him. We arranged to meet for a tour. Another historical irony—I was giving him a tour of a place that, despite his family's absolutely essential part in its construction and prosperity, he had never seen.

That day, I was quite nervous. I didn't want to misspeak or insult or offend. I didn't know how Joe would react, if he'd be angry or sad or bored or overjoyed. Now that I know him better, I know there's this quiet calm that he abides in—a sense that all is well, no matter what. But I didn't know that then.

To support me, Dad came along. We got in my car and headed up to the big house over the hill from Dad's. I stopped in the driveway just in front of the French doors and began telling Joe the history of this place. The hunting lodge in 1725, the three plantations divided, the first year we can prove enslaved people had been here—1781. Then, we drove on. Through the largest plantation—past the big house and down to the barn that the slaves built as practice for building the main house. I pointed out the columns on the front of the barn—the ones that match the portico on the front of the house—and the fact that all the barn's arches are different since they mimic the various arches on the house. Joe nodded, quiet, taking it into himself.

We circled back to Lower Bremo and turned off onto the gravel drive that leads to the cemetery. "This is the slave graveyard," I said. Then, we opened our doors and walked across the grass into the yard proper. I told Joe about Primus and explained to him how the rise and fall of the ground indicated where graves were. As we strolled, he asked about the walls, and Dad told him we hoped to enclose the space again, to mark it more formally as sacred. Joe nodded.

We approached Ben's stone, and my voice quieted. I stood behind it and said, "This is your four-times great-grandfather Ben Creasy's stone." Joe knelt down to read it, laid his hands on the sandstone. Exhaled.

"Ben Creasy," he read. "Aged 18 . . . what does this dash mean?"

"It means the person who carved the stone didn't know exactly what year Ben died, probably because he didn't know exactly what year it was. 18 something."

"Aged 54," he continued. "He was only 54 when he died?"

I nodded. "I can leave you alone for a few minutes if you'd like."

"No, that's okay," he said and smiled up at me with his perfect white teeth and soft eyes. "So this is my great-great-great-great-grandfather. What did you say he did again?"

"He was a carpenter. Ben was a carpenter."

A few minutes later, we settled at my dad's dining room table over tea, talking about the plantation. I showed him documents that listed his ancestors, and he told me about his family who lived over at the edge of the land that makes up these plantations.

"There's a gap in the fence there called 'Lucy's Gap,' 'Lucy's Gate,'" Joe said. "I wonder, could that be named for Lucy from here, Jesse's wife."

"I don't know, but it seems reasonable. I'll see what I can find out."

It seems that the gate is probably named for Lucy Creasy, Joe's great-aunt, Ben's great-granddaughter and also the great-granddaughter of Jesse and another Lucy. Jesse and Lucy's daughter Lavinia Ann married Ben and Judy's son Anthony, Joe's great-great-grandfather.

Joe is descended from two of the most documented families here, a double descendant. More than many African Americans, then, Joe can know his story. Not all of it, not even most of it, but more of it. Two of three marked graves in the cemetery commemorate the lives of his ancestors.

Now, when I walk in that graveyard, I tell Ben about how Joe nearly killed me as I tried to follow him to Applebee's one Thursday afternoon, how he lives in a building so tall that I could see light for miles, how he smells of sandalwood, and how his smile is now part of my story, too. I tell him Joe is my friend.

When I introduce Ben to people who come to see this place and hear the story of its people, I say, "This is Ben Creasy, my friend Joe's four-times great-grandpa." I think Ben smiles.

JESSE NICHOLAS SKIPWITH

Cobbler and hostler. Husband of Lucy. Father of Gerry, Jasper, John, Peyton, George, Lavinia Ann, Jesse, and Erasmus. Born 1775. Died 1838.

JUST WRITING Jesse's name confuses me because I don't know which surname he used. On his letters to The General, Jesse's son Peyton uses the last name Skipwith, so I assume that Jesse might have been a Skipwith as well. Of course, this could be an erroneous assumption, but since I have nothing by way of records to clarify, it's the assumption I'm going to use. Such is the nature of research on enslaved people in the antebellum U.S.

Of course, there is a gravestone in the cemetery with the name Jesse Nicholas. The date on that stone is 1834 (just four years different than the date I have found for Jesse's death), and so it could be Jesse Skipwith's stone, just listed under his wife's surname, or it could be their son's stone. My best hypothesis is that the stone belongs to his son Jesse and that Jesse Sr. is buried somewhere else here at Bremo, maybe even in an unmarked grave in the master's family cemetery, near his wife, Lucy.

Jesse was a shoemaker; the inventory from roughly 1834 through 1840 makes that clear. He turned skin from a cow raised here and made it into coverings for the feet of the people he loved and maybe some that he didn't. My great-grandfather, my mother's grandfather, was a cobbler, too; we have his cobbling box, the tiny horn on the top where he set the shoe as he soled it, as he worked the leather into suppleness. When I see it, I think of Grandpa Joe and Jesse. The Italian immigrant by choice, the African immigrant by force.

Jesse was also the hostler, the horse wrangler, the cattle driver. He raised and cared for the large livestock here. I wonder if he sat at the edge of the pasture, watching the cows and working a piece of leather into a tongue. He must have been a true horseman if he was the man the master chose to care for his thoroughbreds. In my mind, Jesse stands next to Roebuck, the master's most prized sire, and brushes him, tells him about the day and the dailiness of the farm—who was mad at whom and who was expecting a baby soon, whose people were missing, and who was traveling on some errand. A groom's brush in hand, combing Roebuck until his black coat shined. The horse nickers when Jesse hands him an apple as he leaves the stall.

In the center of the Lower Bremo dining room is a picture of the master astride Roebuck. This print was made from the original that is held by the White House. When I gaze at it, I stare at the horse, not because I know one lick about horses, but because I see Jesse's work there in that glossy coat and shimmering bridle. I wonder what our first black president sees when he looks at the portrait.

Jesse was a Christian, a "professor," to use the master's term to describe someone who professed Christianity. He, at least publicly, ascribed to the tenets of Christian faith that the master prescribed. This profession may be why Jesse was chosen to be the Upper Bremo foreman, a position he held quite briefly and then gave back to his master, happier to labor rather than supervise. I can't blame him for this—animals and shoes do what you want, mostly. They can be herded or stored in piles. They usually remain where they are left. People are not like this.

I imagine Jesse on a cold night, walking into the stables feeling the warm, damp breath of the horses. He runs his hands over their flanks and feels them settle against him. Hears the huffs and whinnies of contentment as they take one more turn to grind the wheat his family harvested. His hands soft and strong, he rubs them down from hard rides and talks them into relaxation after days on muddy roads. He picks up a foot and checks a shoe, trims a hoof. Maybe some nights he stood there, without people, and sighed long. So tired. So sore. So worn. The days of hard rides worn into his flesh, too.

I watch him walk the road from the stables to the house, confident that Lucy and his children will be there, tucked in for the night just as his horses and cows are. He walks in, takes off his shoes, and feels eight pairs of arms hug his neck. He eases over to Lucy and rests his chin on her shoulder as she finishes the stew on the fire. He doesn't speak.

The children chatter away over dinner—about lessons and work and the fox they saw with her kits in the false bank above the river. Lucy and Jesse smile and nod, quiet in their listening. I imagine these were good times, all of them together in their own small room, a fire warm on an October night. A day of good work behind them.

In bed, later, Lucy sighs quietly into his shoulder. It doesn't matter whose name they use—they are together, a family, warm.

LUCY NICHOLAS

Nurse. Wife of Jesse Nicholas Skipwith. Mother of George, Peyton, Lavinia Ann, Jesse, Erasmus, Gerry, Jasper, and John. Born 1782. Died 1852.

LUCY WORKED as the nurse at Upper Bremo. She was the woman who nursed the master's children with her own milk—the duty which explains why we use this term to connote the feeding of children, and the caretaker of them, giving us the words *nursery* and our use of the word *nurse* to describe someone who cares for other people.

She gave birth to at least seven, but probably eight children of her own. It's hard to know even this from the spotty records. Her husband, Jesse, was the cobbler and coachman for the master. All 10 of them lived in what was a small house across from the building called the "hotel" in those times. The hotel still stands— at least I think it's that building—just behind what was the latrine (the three holes are still there) and is now the garage at Upper Bremo. I have climbed the stairs that branch to reach the two rooms on the second floor, and I have looked down the hill to where Lucy and Jesse's house might have stood. They lived close to the big house because they were house servants, the people that the master and his family would have called at any time of the day or night if they needed help. I imagine Lucy was there helping when Anne gave birth to all of the master's children. I imagine she was there again when Anne passed so young.

When I imagine her breastfeeding little John and Charles and Sally Cocke, I picture the contrast between the bright brownness of her nipple as it enters their ruby mouths and their white cheeks against her skin laid bare, and I see beauty. I don't want to notice the difference between the two of them, the contrast in their skin color, but I don't know how not to. I don't know how to see that image in that time—Lucy in a rocker in the second-floor bedroom of the big house that overlooks the James River—and not see how gorgeous and inconsistent it was for slave owners to make enslaved people—make black people—perform a most intimate act of nourishment and physical closeness when to eat at the same table was so abhorrent. I don't know how to imagine that and not see color.

Of course, I am looking 150 years later, from a lens that must gaze back through the riots that erupted when black people wanted to swim in the same pools as whites, when blacks battled for the right to sit where they wanted on the bus and attend the same schools. Maybe my lens is corrupted by all the hate we laid on skin color when what Lucy lived through was not only about pigment but also about property. I don't think it's any better from where she looked out—worse, I know—but it is different, I imagine.

I simply can't imagine her in that rocker, a baby latched to her, rocking slowly and singing—I think she'd be singing—and not see the irony in that. The beautiful, prophetic irony.

I wish I knew how Lucy felt about this. I can imagine her loving the chance to be with these children—pristine babies, not yet taught to judge or loathe or fear—in a way so identical to the way she loved her own children. I can imagine her taking the love of these children and honoring it, honoring them with her kindness and respect, with the gifts of her words, her time, her body.

She formed a part of these children. From my 21st-century desk chair, I know that her antibodies became theirs. Her biology moved into their bloodstreams and helped keep them safe. The food she ate entered them, and because she gave to them in this way, she may have suffered for that. Her body wan, her energy weak when she most needed it.

Her children, the children made half from her very own cells, needed care, too. I wonder if they suffered. It seems impossible to me that a woman could nurse four children at the same time, and yet, the master's children and her children were all so young, still so dependent on Lucy's milk. I see her—during these years—rail thin, her hip bones protruding against the one dress she had to wear in pregnancy and out. I hope the master gave her extra food, showed her extra care. I do not know that he would have, though, not out of neglect but just out of apathy, ignorance, willful or not.

Still, the master singularly demonstrated the way he valued Lucy. When Lucy died in 1852, he and his daughter rushed back to Bremo from Belmead Plantation, more than a day's ride away. He wanted "to pay the last offices of respect to the remains of this Christian woman." I like to think it was his desire to make the trip, that he appreciated Lucy so much, that he knew how she had kept his family going even after his wife died.

It's easier, though, for me to see his daughter begging him to go home, the young woman who had grown so attached to this woman who raised her after her mother died, who continued to care for her when her stepmother arrived, the only consistent mother in the land of dead moms and stepmothers. And yet, maybe I am wishful, deluded. Maybe Sally didn't care at all. Maybe I just miss my own mom.

Maybe it was the master's own esteem or maybe the influence of Sally and the other children that brought about this most remarkable act of admiration in Lucy's story: the master had Lucy buried in the family cemetery at Bremo Recess, the smallest of the three plantations. Her grave sits in the corner of the graveyard, next to Sally's. Her headstone is a simple, unmarked piece of slate. She rests now just 8 feet from her master.

It is easy, given the physical proximity of Bremo to Jefferson's Monticello, to want to make more of Lucy's burial site—to read "relations" if not "relationship," if not "rape," into this fact. But I have no evidence for such a thing. I do know that the master at Bremo found Jefferson's relationship with Sally Hemings to be abhorrent—he said so in a much-quoted letter. But whether his disdain was hypocritical—I have no way of knowing.

What I do know is that at Lucy's funeral, everyone at Bremo stopped work and processed to her grave. I see them as they walk down the cart road, all the field hands as cleaned up as they can be, the house slaves in their finest clothing and shined shoes. Ben made the pine casket that rests on the horse wagon that Jesse drives. The people follow. They sing as they walk, or at least I imagine they do, because this is what I hope for. They walk 2 miles, the same distance I traverse in less than five minutes in my car, and gather around her grave as their master says a few words.

"We may all well implore that our last end may be like hers," he wrote in his journal. I hope he said this at her grave.

For all her apparent importance, it took me more than nine months of research to find out that Lucy was in this cemetery.

Her name is not etched into the stone like Sally's and not like the master's. No one in the Cocke family today knew she was buried there. Only one person suggested I might look for the cemetery plat to see the names of the slaves buried in the family cemetery. When I found this small piece of paper tucked into one of the 195 boxes of the collection at UVA, I almost wept. There—Lucy, nurse. A hand-drawn sketch her only marker.

Lucy's children lived into emancipation. Her son Peyton and his family traveled to Liberia, her son George and his family went to Alabama, and her daughter Lavinia Ann married Anthony Creasy and became the mother of Oliver, who is the three-times great-grandfather of my friend Joe. So Lucy is Joe's five-times great-grandmother.

Lucy didn't travel far in her life. She was born in Virginia—probably in Surry County—and died here in Bremo. All her 70 years on this land of which she is now a part.

7

A PLACE'S HISTORY

The history of these 3,500 acres where I now sit—the Bremo Plantations in Central Virginia—goes back to 17th-century England, where the Cockes, a wealthy family of English aristocrats, owned an estate that (most people assume) carried the name "Bremo." Sometime during the middle part of that century, the family moved to the colony of Virginia and founded another Bremo down in the Tidewater of the state, Surry County specifically. Two brothers were given land grants there as part of the English colonization effort. Within a few decades, King George I gave Richard and his brother Benjamin another vast tract of land, nearly 6,000 acres, further up the James River, at the south end of what is now Fluvanna County.

To establish this land as owned by king and country, the Cocke brothers had to build a single edifice here. True to the future of their new commonwealth, they ordered the construction of a stone hunting lodge on a hill overlooking the James. The structure was roughly 20 by 12 and still stands today as the dining room of the plantation house near my father's home. It's had a marked upgrade with wide, heart pine floor planks, columns, and powder blue plaster, but the walls—18-inch-thick stone—are original. As far as the record shows, this structure stood alone on the land for the next 50 years or so while the family focused their attention on homes and land in the Tidewater.

In 1780, Hartwell Cocke, son of the original landowner, Richard Cocke, had a child, John Hartwell Cocke, to whom he left the upstate land on his death when John was a mere 12 years old. John's uncle, another Richard, became his guardian, raised the boy, and sent him off to university at the College of William and Mary when John was 14 years old. Upon graduation, John began to establish his own life, taking up residence at Mount Pleasant Plantation in Surry with the enslaved people his father left him in his will.

In roughly 1781, Richard, John's guardian, began sending slaves to prepare the land at Bremo, presumably on behalf of John. Then, in the early 1800s, John and his young wife, Anne Blaws Barraud Cocke, started splitting their time between Surry and Fluvanna Counties. In roughly 1801, John ordered the construction of a house called "Recess," where they lived for the next few years and had their children—John Hartwell III and Louisiana Barraud—before moving in 1808 to Upper Bremo, the Monticello-like house that became the main plantation.

About 15 years later, Cocke directed his slaves to add on to the original hunting lodge, now on the farm called Lower Bremo (the farm, incidentally, where I was raised), and made it a residence for his son Cary Charles Cocke. During these years, Anne and John also had one more son, Phillip St. George, and two more daughters, Anne Blaws and Sallie Faulcon. Anne died, to John's great sorrow, in 1816, less than 10 years after her plantation home was complete.

During these early years in Fluvanna, John formally divided his Bremo property into three distinct plantations—Bremo Recess, Lower Bremo, and Upper Bremo (or simply Bremo), a division that remains intact to this day. Each plantation operated separately with its own enslaved workforce, overseer, and farm structures. When people visit these properties now, it's the structures they notice. They marvel at the houses and sigh at the barns. As one friend said, "It's like a plantation ghost town here," and it is. It's as if one day a vast wind or virulent plague swept through and took all the people. Of course, John might very well have felt this very thing had happened with emancipation. But I'm getting ahead of myself.

Early on in his adult life, John earned a good reputation as a farmer and experimental agriculturist. He came to abhor tobacco —calling it the "Devil's plant"—at a time when tobacco was the mainstay of Virginia crops. Instead, he grew corn, tried cotton, and even went so far as to plant mulberry trees as a way of cultivating silkworms for production. He believed in vigilant crop rotation and was one of the first people in the U.S. to use terracing for gardens. His notes (archived at the University of Virginia, an institution for which he served on the very first Board of Visitors) show complex plans for orchards and vegetables gardens, and his notes on marling—using a clay-based form of fertilizer—are quite detailed, much to my tired eyes' dismay. It is for his agricultural ingenuity as much as anything else that he is lauded.[1]

John's additional claim to fame—if he has one in the history of America writ larger than Virginia or Fluvanna County—is that he earned the title of brigadier general during the War of 1812. I am not a military historian, nor do I want this work to divert into a study of military prowess, so I will leave this information as the only reference here.Let it suffice to say that because of his military experience, for the rest of history—at least here on the Bremo farms—this man will be called "The General," and so I will call him.

Influenced by his second wife, Louisa, whom he married in 1821,

The General came to detest alcohol and took on the temperance movement as one of his great passions. In fact, the couple's zeal for temperance was so great that they constructed a "Temperance Fountain" and placed it on the banks of the James and Kanawha Canal, the main waterway between Richmond and points west, so that bargemen could refresh themselves with water rather than alcohol. (Of course the family joke is the sailors used the water to mix their mint juleps. No teetotalers, these modern Cockes.)

The death of Anne and his marriage to Louisa were also deeply influential in The General's religious life. While it seems he would have called himself a Christian throughout his years, it was his marriage to Louisa that pushed him to be what can only be called staunch in his faith. In fact, his views on the Sabbath were so devout that the only activities he permitted his family on Sunday were reading from Scripture and church attendance.

This viewpoint extended beyond the walls of his house as well. The slaves were expected to keep the Sabbath, and to that end, The General brought in a preacher most Sundays to share with the people "a lesson." On the Sundays when a preacher was not available, one of the enslaved men or The General himself might give a sermon.

Perhaps the greatest testament to The General's religious zeal is the still-standing slave chapel that he had built in 1835 on the property line between Lower and Upper Bremo. The one-room building stood just up the road from the slave cemetery and was the regular meetinghouse for not only slaves but also the Cocke family and their guests on occasion. In the present day, the chapel serves as the parish hall for Grace Episcopal Church in Bremo Bluff, the town just down the river. This building needed to be repaired because it was moving quickly toward ruin. The Cocke family and the church chose to move it off the plantation, an action which saved the building.

In addition to his great crusades against tobacco and alcohol and his deep devotion to Christianity, The General was extremely invested in the cause of African colonization. As a founding member of the American Colonization Society (ACS), General Cocke helped to purchase land in the western portion of the African continent that would become, in time, the country of Liberia. The ACS's great mission was to purchase slaves from their owners, free them, and then transport those freed people to Liberia. The idea was to colonize the continent of Africa for Christ with these freed people, hence the name Liberia. For The General, this was the best—and perhaps the only—acceptable resolution to a system that was economically and politically flawed.

It's clear from his writings that The General saw problems with the system of slavery. He believed a slave-based economy encouraged sloth and lack of motivation among poor whites and, thus, discouraged the overall advancement of the American economy. He also believed that the system was tyrannical in that it kept the United States beholden to the vicissitudes of the slave trade. While he may have also held some moral reservations about "the peculiar institution," his reasons for supporting colonization had less to do with the treatment of enslaved people and much more to do with the sustenance of the American economy.

In fact, The General did not believe that freed slaves could survive in mainstream American society; he felt that white and black people could not abide together civilly. I cannot say why he held this belief. Perhaps he thought white society would not accept freed slaves as full members of their world. It's possible he thought that freed slaves would never be able to support themselves with trades. Maybe being an eyewitness to the resulting subjugation and oppression of slaves led to that conclusion. A more common reason would be that The General held some encultured and deeply rooted racist leanings. I expect his conclusions about separated races arose from some blend of these ideas. Or perhaps his encultured racism gave rise to the other reasons to justify his thoughts and actions.

Whatever the ideas behind his belief, despite his distaste for the slave system, The General did not support abolition. In fact, he opposed it quite emphatically. He believed, moreover, that taking the hard-line stance in favor of abolition against other Southerners who not only accepted but advocated for slavery would result in civil war. With the hindsight of history, it's easy to see he was correct in this assessment.

So rather than work for abolition, he began to work for what historians have dubbed "gradual emancipation," a process that stipulated, among other things, that the newly freed people be part of a massive colonization effort. Beginning in the 1830s, he started emancipating his slaves if they agreed to move to Liberia immediately upon receipt of their free papers.

To receive this "gift" of emancipation, the men and women enslaved on the Bremo plantations had to meet several conditions: profession of Christianity, a pledge of temperance, progress in becoming literate (able to read if not to write). Additionally, the men had to learn a skilled trade. Failure to subscribe to and achieve these requirements meant continued enslavement.

In total, The General freed fewer than 35 people over the course of 30 years or so. In contrast, other members of the ACS freed (or, to be more specific, took payment from ACS for) all their enslaved people. Why The General's numbers are so low, I can only speculate, but my best hypothesis is that he deemed them not ready for freedom. Certainly he found some people "worthy" of this opportunity, and so I cannot find him simply hypocritical; I cannot conclude that he was in favor of freeing people for colonization while not actually participating in the process.

Considering the standards by which he deemed someone "ready" helps me understand his thought process.

The requirements were rigorous, and The General's standards for achieving them rigid. Perhaps he made achievement so difficult because he was dictatorial, because he could not loosen his strict sense of moral and religious order, because he—consciously or subconsciously—feared losing his workforce, or because he felt these things necessary for success as free people. It's possible to locate some of the responsibility in the enslaved people themselves; maybe choosing to be "free" was not worth the cost of leaving one's extended family and the country which—for all the Bremo slaves—was the only home they had ever known. They may have deliberately failed to live up to these standards. While I cannot know the full reality of any of these choices, even with an extensive collection of documents to inform me, my hypothesis is that both The General and the enslaved people at Bremo had reasons for not wanting emancipation to come by way of Liberia. It would be easy for me to indict The General alone—to hold him entirely responsible, to label him racist and selfish, to write him off. But I can't do that. Nothing is ever that simple, even in hindsight.

The General was, more than many slave owners, a kind master, as the surviving documents—including handwritten letters from the slaves—seem to confirm. He taught the slave children to read and write, sometimes at the risk of his own physical safety. (Because he taught his slaves to read and write, The General was nearly beaten to death in a nearby town.) He trained the enslaved men in many trades—masonry, blacksmithing, carpentry—and all the records indicate that the slaves were well fed and well housed, at least by the standards applied to enslaved people in that time. He regularly sought medical care for them, and at least once, he traveled hundreds of miles to attend a funeral for a slave. On some level, then, he truly cared for these people. I certainly wouldn't excuse his actions or practices, but again, these were complex times, and it seems The General was a complex man.

But of course, these "kindnesses" were not simply gifts. All the skills enslaved people learned helped provide The General with income from their "hiring out" as well as saved him money from having to hire someone to perform those tasks. Additionally, strong, healthy workers meant more productivity and less expense. Thus, his care of them was probably directed by, at best, mixed motives and, at worst, singular self-regard. Also, when enslaved people did not behave according to his strict standards, rules he laid out in detail in some of his many writings on the subject, they were subject to whipping, sale, and "turning out."

This last punishment was perhaps the most harsh. Given The General's professed belief that formerly enslaved people would not be able to support themselves in white society, coupled with the fact that a black person without papers—either a traveling pass from a master or legal documents showing their freedom— was in danger of sale or even murder, "turning out" could be, in fact, worse than simply being sold.

These considerations make it difficult for me to see him as "the benevolent master," though I recognize that by the standards of his day he was regarded as such, even by the people he owned.

In his older years, The General lost his second wife and his youngest son, Phillip St. George. His health also began to fail, and in the final years of his life, he and his son Cary swapped houses, The General choosing instead to live in the smaller, more manageable Lower Bremo.

As the Civil War moved like a torrent though the country, The General's ideas about slavery took a turn. It seems that the war caused him to assume a hard line on the institution, one he had equivocated on his whole life, and this makes me sad in a profound way. He entrenched himself in the South's proslavery stance and threw his allegiance wholeheartedly to the Confederacy. But of course, my view here, too, oversimplifies, even if it is my true feeling.

It's easy to see how—as a Southern planter—this could happen and yet, still, I am grieved by this fact. I wish he had found the moral courage to take the side of freedom. He stood against the Southern aristocracy on tobacco but couldn't bring himself to do so on slavery, even for the lives of the very people he lived with day in and day out. Perhaps this position, more than anything, shows his true feelings on the institution. Or perhaps it only shows his allegiance to the place and culture he called home.

In 1866, just the year after he saw all his slaves freed, The General died in his bedroom at Lower Bremo. Sometimes I go in that room and look at his bed and dressers, which still furnish the space. I stand next to the bed with his headboard that almost reaches to the 10-foot ceiling, and I lay my hand there. I want to feel him in this wood, to believe that objects hold memories as all the ghost shows say they do. I want to know his life and the way it passed to death. I want to find a way to uncover something certain about his feelings for the people he owned, even as I know that if he flickered to me in these moments, a full body in his dressing gown of death, I would still have my doubts.

But still, I wonder. I wonder what he thought as he lay ill in that bed. I wonder if he had regrets or felt pride. I wonder who he remembered, Louisa and Anne, his children, Primus, Malvina, Lucy. This, too, I cannot know.

There is a story I've heard, though, passed along through mouths and ears for almost 150 years now, a story that says The General committed suicide and that the free people who had stayed to work for him were sworn to secrecy of this fact by his children. I can't know if this is true, and I don't really know if it matters. But it seems to speak of a quiet judgment. By whom is the real question.

I, for one, hope it isn't true. I owe this man—just as I owe the people he owned—my sense of home, and while a great part of me wants to condemn him with a righteous anger, another part of me only wishes him well. For what can come of bitterness and anger at a dead man but bitterness and anger.

So I hope, in the end—with freedom still so large with promise for the people he no longer owned—he felt peace.

8

LETTY TOMPKINS AND LETTY GAULT

Letty Tompkins. Cook. Wife of unknown. Born before 1791.
Died date unknown.
Letty Gault. Field hand. Wife of unknown. Born 1795. Died
date unknown.

THESE TWO WOMEN with the same name weave in and out of my
research so closely that I cannot always discern who is whom.
Sometimes, I think I have a fact about one of them pinned down
—a relation, a location, some reference to their work—and then I
find no, that information applies to the other Letty. Or wait,
maybe it is this Letty. I lose track of which Letty is which all the
time.

Letty Tompkins was one of those people who are often listed
among the other "single" people at Bremo. On an inventory
taken sometime between 1834 and 1840, her entry reads, "Letty
Tompkins—Recess—P—Husband owned by T. Shores 2 Grandchildren Morgan and Addison." The man who owned her
husband, Thomas Shores, ran a plantation just on the west side

of Bremo; his name is now glittering on a road sign (Shores Road) where his plantation once stood. When people tell you they live over at Shores, this is what they mean. These people are usually black.

On the inventory of families, Letty Gault's entry says, "Letty— UB—NP—lives with Mother. Husband sold—FH—1 child hired out." I do not know who her husband was or who hired her daughter. Her mother was named Hannah, and Hannah was a spinner who was one of the original slaves that The General brought to Bremo from Surry County. Letty's father was named Dick, and she had eight siblings—Sam, Mourning, Katy, Isham, Miama and Julyann (twins), and Jesse.

It is possible that Letty Tompkins (I'm tempted to say Letty T. and Letty G. as we did when we had two Jennifers in our third-grade class) saw her husband at the Shores Plantation. It wouldn't have been impossible since she could have gotten a Sunday pass or perhaps just met up with him on the property line that joined Shores Plantation with Bremo. At Christmas, her daughter probably came home, too. Maybe The General let her husband join them here at Bremo for the day. Maybe they celebrated together. It could almost sound ideal.

In 1843, The General hires a man named Andrew Maxwell to oversee the work and garden at Recess. As part of that arrangement, The General states that Maxwell will have a certain number of "hands."

To perform these duties, the following hands will be exclusively under said Maxwell's direction. Isaac the Gardner, the boy, Polly the milk woman, Polly the cook, and the following named will at all intervals between the times of the duties in the House, render services in the gardens truc, patches, yard, lawn, etc, etc— Solomon, Addison and Letty.

(The document continues, without a hint of irony, to say that

Maxwell will be paid $150 a year plus room and board "in consideration of the above duties." It does not, of course, say anything about pay for Letty or her colleagues.) This woman who works and lives at Recess is almost certainly Letty Tompkins since this inventory lists her as living at Recess. The fact that Addison, Letty Tompkins's grandson, is also there seems to confirm this fact. If so, the Tompkinses were favored enough to be trusted away from the main house.

But if The General showed some sort of favor for Letty Tompkins's family, Letty Gault's family seems to have been out of favor with him. He didn't often sell people away, and yet, Letty's husband was sold. Her daughter was hired out. It's almost as if Letty was punished by having her family taken away, although I doubt anyone at the time—besides perhaps Letty herself— would have seen it that way. But it's not just Letty who receives less than favorable attention from The General and the men who oversee his plantations. After Isham and Julyann are moved to Alabama with 48 other people in the late 1830s, they are both beaten by George Skipwith, the enslaved man who acted as The General's overseer. George claimed that Isham was lazy and that Julyann had misplaced her hoe, but I can't help but wonder if part of the reason they received this treatment was because George had absorbed some of his master's opinion of the family.

These scant facts and the seeming favoritism and antagonism of The General form all I know about either Letty. The only other scraps I have are a couple of dates where one or the other of them (I can't always tell which) receives a blanket or is included on an inventory.

It is so easy for me to conflate these two women—to make their two lives tell one story—for a couple of important reasons: they were not that far apart in age, and they both had husbands who did not work here on the farm and were, thus, not listed on inventories. I pulled much of the basis for my profiles from a key inventory that was made in the 1830s, and for most people, a spouse is listed. Without that information or a wide gap in age, it's so simple to mix these women up and assume they are one person.

To do so, would, of course, mean that their individual lives are not important, that their individual identities are so insignificant that to reduce them to a composite is enough. Thus, I try to take extra care to ensure I am thinking, speaking, writing about the right Letty at the right time.

Still, sometimes I want to shake all these inventories or rip them apart in frustration. I get so weary of hunting so hard for the tiniest scrap of information. Sometimes it feels as if I'm trying to catch fireflies with a net. I only see the facts of these people's lives for the briefest moments, and when I do see them, their stories often slip through holes stitched big by the legacy of a system that says, "Letty Gault or Letty Tompkins, what does it matter as long as they do their work and abide their place?"

Then, though, I see Letty Tompkins's face glow with the golden light of a thousand lightning bugs as she walks in from the Recess garden. I see Letty Gault's calloused hands tuck her elderly mother, Hannah, in at night in the room they share. At those moments, well, then, all the swinging of that big net feels like holy work.

9

GRUFF

Son of Aggy. Brother of Daphne. Uncle of Minerva. Born August 1794. Died date unknown.

GRUFF IS one of those people whose stories sound so fascinating when first spoken but fade like an echo into the gray of history.

I know he was born in August 1794 because his birth is listed on an inventory of births to enslaved women. The other side of the inventory lists The General's dog litters. When I first saw this document, I was almost gleeful because it seemed to give me a long, long list of names—maybe kinship connections for people who had been alone to me thus far. But then, when I found these were dogs—listed in the same hand and the same manner as humans . . . To say I was horrified is to not say enough. It's a bitter and harsh document that brings an ache to my stomach every time it flips up in my stacks of research.

Gruff's mother was Aggy. There were at least two women named Aggy at Bremo—Black Aggy and Aggy Smith—and I do not know which of these women was Gruff's mother.

After his birth, Gruff disappears from the records for 17 years. In 1811, according to researcher Boyd Coyner, he was sent to a white weaver to learn the trade of weaving and tailoring. To be placed as an apprentice, a person had to have earned the trust and respect of The General. This opportunity—as The General would have seen it and as it was in many ways—required a slave to be away from the plantation for a good bit of time. In most cases it required the owner to pay the person who was training the slave. This was not a casual investment for The General. Gruff's training in this area saved the plantation money since they did not have to pay for premade fabric or hire outside weavers. It was also an opportunity for other plantation owners to hire Gruff for their weaving work.

Finally, having a trade in The General's system gave the enslaved an opportunity to earn his emancipation, not only by purchasing it but also by proving his ability to support himself. Thus, Gruff's selection for this apprenticeship indicates The General's esteem for him and belief in Gruff's potential.

But after this brief reference in 1811, I don't have any further information about Gruff for almost 40 years. Perhaps there are a few references tucked into documents that I have missed or not yet read, but in terms of the major events of Bremo—the emancipation of people to Liberia, the migration of some 50 people to Alabama—Gruff is absent.

Then, on an inventory dated between 1834 and 1840, he appears again, this time at Recess, where he is listed as a "non-professor" and a field hand. There's also a note that says, "wife at Fuqua's." Most likely the Fuqua mentioned is John or Joseph Fuqua, a plantation owner here in Fluvanna with whom The General probably had business or less formal connections. The Fuqua plantation was at least a few miles away from Bremo.

In any case, even if Gruff's wife were just a few miles away, he still probably would have only seen her on Sundays, the one day when the slaves had a break from work. These days, he had to wait until after church and then walked—or had her walk to Bremo—to see her. At best, their visits would have been a few hours long. I find it hard to imagine maintaining a marriage with that little time together, but then I find it hard to imagine what it means to be prohibited to live with your spouse because another human being owns her.

If I speculate about Gruff's life, about the fact that it seems, even after being trained as a weaver, he came back to being a field hand, the lowest "rank" of any slave on the plantation, I could postulate about what that means in terms of his ability to weave, or his behavior, or The General's fickleness. But I won't.

Somehow, here, it seems important to leave Gruff's story bare, unadorned with much of my imagination, because Gruff's story is the story of so many American slaves. Their written histories are sparse with fact. While they were the people upon whose labor we built this country—the foundation of the men we call the Founding Fathers—we have so little we can learn about them.

Yet, they are crucial. We would not have Bremo or Monticello or Montpelier or Mount Vernon. We would not have The General or Jefferson or Madison or Washington, as we understand them, without their slaves. It was the work of their enslaved people that gave them the time and the freedom, in the full weight of irony, to build this nation. If they had needed to build their own homes or plow their own fields, our country would look much different now than it does.

That is not to say, in any way, that slavery was "worth it" or even "necessary." I will never believe that. But slavery was and is a fact, and its presence helped shaped our nation, for all our good and all our lingering ill.

To be able to list what I know of Gruff, one of the people who quite literally helped build our country, is a blessing. That his life is reduced to less than a half sheet of paper makes my heart crinkle. He deserves a full story, not just three facts.

Gruff was a man with few choices, no legal standing, no ability to even travel at his will. Yet, he was a man. With affections and demeanor. With a particular kind of walk. With aches and tales.

Yet, because of slavery, his story is reduced to this. Three facts. Not enough. Not ever.

10

NED EDWARDS

Coachman. Husband of Felicia. Father of Lucy and Berthier.
Born 1800. Died 1862.

A MAN NAMED Ned is included on tithe lists for Fluvanna County (documents that showed when plantation owners had paid their tithe to the Anglican church) from the 1780s. He's listed on a later inventory as being in Surry County in February 1791, which is odd since he seems to have been in Fluvanna then, too, but maybe he traveled between the two plantations. One month later, in March 1791, his name appears on the inventory for The General's Bear Garden Plantation, across the river from Bremo, with several other people who had been moved up the James River from Surry to Central Virginia.

Then, in September, another Ned appears on the records, born to a woman named Diniri. Maybe this baby is Ned Sr.'s son. In 1798, Ned's name comes up in Surry County records next to the name of an enslaved man named Hercules; I'm assuming this is Ned Sr. since the Ned Jr. would only be seven and, therefore, unlikely to travel. The 1801 "Inventory taken of John H Cocke's Estate at Bremo" lists Ned Jr. as one of the children on plantation number 1, which would be Recess, given the year. In 1806, his name appears on a list of plantation expenses when he "went to Smithfield to pay ferryage." This man could be either Ned Sr. or Ned Jr. since by age 15, a young enslaved man might be running errands for his owner.

But it's the baby I know. Ned Edwards, Ned Jr. As with many things, I am making an assumption, taking an educated guess that perhaps the first Ned is Ned Edwards's father. Maybe that man used the surname Edwards as well. Maybe he used Cocke. Maybe he had an entirely different surname altogether. Or maybe Ned is just a derivative of Edwards, a nickname for a surname. The name that Ned Edwards's mother whispered to him when he was sleeping in her arms—that name we will never know. It's lost to the brutality of slavery.

It is the names of people that are, perhaps, the hardest to pin down. It is the names of people that often yield the most information, if I can pin them to a person and place that pin into facts across time.

Many people believe that all enslaved people here in the U.S. took or were given the names of their owners, but this simply wasn't the case. While no enslaved person was legally allowed a surname (just as they were not legally allowed to marry), many families did take last names, and only rarely were those names those of their owners. What makes this research more complicated is that sometimes, as in the case of the Skipwiths, it appears they carried the name of another slave-owning family (the white Skipwiths were very prominent in Richmond) or that the family chose a name whose origins are untraceable, like Edwards. After emancipation, some formerly enslaved people chose entirely new surnames, muddying the trail of names even as they made their own identities clearer, more their own.

Thus, when I'm reading inventories and see Ned, I have to examine dates and work histories. I need to determine if the person listed is the same person that I am researching at that moment or if this name might refer to another person entirely, perhaps the first Ned's child or someone else altogether. As we still do now, enslaved people often named their children after other members of their community, people they admired. Of course, on some plantations—although this does not seem to be the case at Bremo—the owner also named his "new property." Thus, names in this research are fraught with ambiguity, confusion, and hints about both genealogical connections and power relationships.

About Ned Edwards, I do know this much. He was a house servant, and historian Randall Miller came to the conclusion that he was The General's coachman, the man who drove the carriage while two postilions—Billy and Phil—rode the horses themselves. As always, these positions were given only to the most trusted slaves since these men held The General's very life and sometimes wealth in their hands.

I don't have much more specific information about Ned at all.

So I turn to my imagination and see a tall man, thin with ramrod posture. He's wearing a waistcoat and a high collar. Perhaps I have pinched this vision of him from the cardboard cutout I saw of Thomas Jefferson's "man" Burwell when I visited Monticello, but this is the picture that comes to mind when I imagine Ned. He is, of course, more finely dressed than the field hands and even the other house servants since he is regularly in the public eye. He wears a coat, and his hair is impeccably trimmed, his face clean-shaven.

Perfect manners are a necessity. The sense and education to know when to open a door for someone, when to bow slightly, when to incline his head at a question without having to speak, all serve him well. His voice is soft but steady. The lilt of the

Virginia Tidewater dropping into the middle of each phrase like a breath. "Yes, sir."

Before dawn, he rises, putting a weighty hand on the shoulder of his son, Berthier, to wake him. While the dew is still heavy on the grass, they make their way to the stables, where they brush down the horses and prepare the tack for The General's trip to Monticello, which will commence shortly after dawn since The General is an early riser. The coach itself is clean and tidy, shiny with black lacquer and solid craftsmanship, a masterpiece created by Ben Creasy's talented hands. Ned takes a clean brush to the red seats inside and brisks them so that the pile stands up evenly. He wipes down his own leather seat before hitching the horses, just two today, no postilions needed.

The General comes out, compliments Ned on his work, and then decides to ride Roebuck to Monticello that day. Ned sighs quietly and pulls the carriage back to the barn, unharnesses the horses, leads them to their stalls, and slips a bridle on Roebuck before bridling a mare for himself. He always accompanies The General on his rides. As he settles a saddle onto Roebuck's massive black back that Jesse Skipwith has so carefully groomed, he slides a piece of sugar against the horse's muzzle. A little insurance that the horse will heed him if need be.

Both men mount and begin the ride 35 miles over the mountain to Mr. Jefferson's place. Ned does not say goodbye to his wife, Felicia. This is a workday, and despite the fact that he may not return for days nor does he know at all when he will return, such sentimentality is not respected by The General in his peers, much less in his "servants." They ride off, mud kicking the back of their boots already. Side by side down the lane, equal in everything except what matters.

Ned died in 1862, just one year before the news of his promised freedom to ride wherever he pleased could reach him.

11

NELSON

Husband of Betsy. Father of Nelson, Peyton, and Eliza. Born about 1810. Died??

THE FIRST MENTION I read of Nelson came in an email from a Charlottesville archaeologist named Steve Thompson. Steve and I are part of an informal research group called the Central Virginia History Researchers, and so he knew about my interest in the slaves from Bremo. He told me that he'd just found a letter from the first University of Virginia anatomy professor talking about a young boy who was enslaved at Bremo, and then he copied in the text:

Xmas 1826

Dear Sir

Nelson has been anxious to go to Bremo for the last week but the weather has prevented him. I am still disposed to retain him in the same service as last year, that is as a stable servant and to attend to my garden as I have been compelled, owing to his inability to do his duties, to remove him from the house.

As he has been unable to see his Master this Xmas I have sent him down to you with this intelligent.

Truly yours

Robley Dunglison

On my first reading of this note, I was shocked by two things—I had no idea university professors kept slaves as servants, a fact that should have been obvious to me. But something about my affinity for universities and my respect for higher education led me to think better of them, to want to see them as beyond the social conventions of their time. The University of Virginia (UVA) was founded, however, by slaveholders, including The General, who was a member of the original Board of Visitors. Because of this, I really shouldn't have been surprised that the professors there used slave labor.

The second thing that caught my breath was that Dunglison seemed to think that Nelson's desire to get back to Bremo was based on his desire to see The General—"he has been unable to see his Master"—rather than to see his own family. I just could not get over the ignorance, prejudice, insensitivity that would lead anyone to think that a young boy's desire to be home would have to do with the man who owned him than with his parents, siblings, or friends. If I give Dunglison the benefit of the doubt, I can see that Nelson might have conveyed his desire to see his master in order to express a more socially acceptable sentiment. Showing too much emotion for his family may have induced scorn. In Nelson's case, he may have been refused his trip back to Bremo.

But somehow I don't think it was simply Nelson's words that spurred this attitude. Anyone who owned slaves, it seems to me, had to believe that the relationship between owner and enslaved was primary, even necessary in some sense. If the enslaved person had been viewed in the context of his own family, he would then have had too much humanity. In other words, it was easier to think of Nelson as a dog who missed his owner rather than as a boy who missed his mama.

This, of course, is entirely conjecture on my part. I don't know if Nelson's mother was even at Bremo.

Dunglison was the first professor of biology and anatomy at the then-new university, and he was also President Jefferson's personal physician. So Nelson was working for an important man. Maybe it's this knowledge that causes me to hear Dunglison's voice as a bit arrogant when I read over it. My own bias against the professor, I expect.

Still, this short letter reveals so much. Nelson has been demoted from Dunglison's house servant to stable and garden boy because of his "inability to do his duties." His demotion could have come about for any number of reasons. Nelson could have been negligent, although if he was, I expect Dunglison would have simply sent him back to Bremo and demanded a return of some of his hiring fee. Perhaps Nelson was simply too young or too physically weak to perform the duties Dunglison required of a house servant. Or maybe he lacked the decorum or the more fair complexion so many people preferred in their house servants. Whatever the case, he wasn't sent home but was kept on to work at UVA as it was built.

It seems, though, that Nelson didn't stay more than another year at UVA. Records indicate that in 1827 he was hired out to Mrs. Jane B. Cary's estate back here in Fluvanna County. John Noll took him on for the Cary estate at the rate of $55 for the year, perhaps as an apprentice in some trade, as Gruff had been.

After that, Nelson disappears from the records until 1840, where he is then listed on an inventory as being between 24 and 36 years old. Two years later, he is on another inventory with the other enslaved men. By 1846, he seems to be married to a woman named Betsy, as their names appear together on a list of tithables for people over 16. His name appears one other time, on an undated inventory with Betsy again and three people—Nelson Jr., Eliza, and Peyton—who I assume to be his children.

Other than these mentions, Nelson doesn't figure much in the records. I don't know what his job on the plantation was. In fact, I don't even know which plantation—Upper Bremo, Lower Bremo, or Recess—he worked on.

I can't help imagining what it must have been like for this young man to come back to rural, isolated Fluvanna County after being a part of the great energy at UVA. I wonder if he was—like so many, like me—built for the country but intrigued by what happened in the city. Or if like many others, maybe he simply loathed city life altogether.

I wonder if he ever visited Monticello with Dunglison when that man attended on the president. I wonder if Nelson perused Jefferson's library while the former president was being treated in the room next door.

I wonder what stories he told when he came back to the farm. Of libraries and learned men. Of lectures on medicine overheard as he cleaned. I wonder if those stories became regular tales that expanded the perspectives of those little ones around his feet. Or if he kept them quiet, folded inside himself, his private memories, some of the few things he actually owned.

12

HEARTHSTONES

S ometimes I don't even see them as I walk past, my arms laden with empty coffee mugs and grocery bags full of organic milk and Cotswold Cheddar. Most days, I just pass them as I do the other things that I pass in my day—unseen unless they have changed.

Stone doesn't change easily. Not unless we make it change.

They sit, these two hearthstones, just to the left of the stairs that lead to my father's house. He has placed them there as monuments. What was here. What can be lost. What can be reclaimed.

Each of them is a waist-high obelisk of sandstone, a shelf turned on end to become memory, not just simple use. Their color is of sunset, all umber and peach and a shade that Crayola has not yet named but sits somewhere beneath our skin and brightens us with joy or exertion.

The space where these stones sat is empty now, hollowed out by excavation, robbed barren by my father when he needed stone for other places on the farm. He didn't know these were slave quarters then, but he carries the sadness of his disruption now.

The pillars, they are monuments to his remembering. His reminder that the whole story has not yet been told. That things which seem to be piles of rubble may be more like memory.

At Upper Bremo, the steps are carved from the same sandstone as the hearthstones. People always marvel at their beauty—the swirls of color still strong even 200 years later. I have yet to hear anyone comment on the size of the stones, about the heft of them. Yet, this is what I always notice, the weight of each one carved to a perfect flatness and then laid, with ropes and shoulders, to its place below my feet.

I picture Jesse and Anthony with feathers (light planks of wood) and wedges on an overcast spring day as they arch their backs over a massive seam of sandstone. They bend perpendicular to the ground and insert the tiny pieces of wood before tapping the wedges down slowly. Then, the next hole 6 inches along and then, the next. Until eventually, the stone splits as if it had meant to be separate from itself all along.

The men do this all day until they have 16 perfect stones to lay in place.

The next morning, Primus calls some of the field hands—maybe Elias or Tom or Robin or Gilbert—to load the stones onto the wagon. The draft horses are hitched to the front, and all the men bend and lift together to place one stone on the bed behind the horses. They then flip it side over side until it comes to rest at the front of the wagon. Three more times for this load.

They walk beside the wagon as it climbs up from the quarry and mounts the hill where the first story of the house is just being bricked over. Carefully, they lift down each stone and roll it again to the steps that were laid the week before. Each man takes his corner, and they pick it up again—hurrying with caution up four steps to set it on end at the top of the portico.

Jesse and Anthony evaluate the piece—how it will lie on the sand and pebbles that form the base, which colors go best in each spot, how to hide the feather-and-wedge grooves from sight. Then, they all pick up the stone again, this time lowering just one corner and then wrapping a rope around the side to slide the piece haltingly down, perfect against the granite that forms the threshold they will never cross.

They work this process for weeks, all the way across the front steps, then up the two side staircases that form the walkways and porches by the breezeways. Everything is perfectly symmetrical when they are done bending.

DAD and I hike down Grandmother's Walk by the slave cemetery and wind our way below the Upper Bremo manager's house. We wend our way to the Temperance Temple with its marble front. We decide to take the back path through the fields to go home.

As we pass the 1950s pump house, Dad kicks aside some leaves to show me sandstone pedestals partially carved to match the column bases just up the hill and out of sight on the big house. These are the leavings from the mason's work. I take pictures.

I want to pick one up and carry it home with me—but I cannot lift it, let alone heft it any distance.

I still hope to get one someday. It will sit on my porch and hold up nothing. It will remind me of where my foundations lie and who I owe them to.

EACH TIME I stop to see the hearthstones tucked into the ground at my father's house, I wonder what their story is. I imagine they are leavings, pieces of the grand slabs left over and carried on a cart to the Lower Bremo barn—almost a mile away—to make a threshold for fire.

I wonder what Jesse and Anthony set on them. Boots to dry. Tiny carved statues for their children to play with. The spoons they used for cooking.

Or maybe these stones were not in the stonemasons' houses at all. Perhaps they were gifts to women whose husbands lived away or to families who did not have access to such fine work. Maybe Anthony and Jesse laid them out carefully, just as thoughtfully as they did at the big house because they were master craftsmen.

I try to picture Jesse carrying a stone almost as tall as his oldest child. I see him climb the path from the Lower Bremo house, past the ice dams and on up the hill to the quarter by the pasture. The red stone first set on his right shoulder, then tucked below his left arm, finally cradled on both forearms for those last few hundred feet. I watch him as on the next Sunday he digs down into the earth by the fireplace and shapes a level slot. I marvel at the stone laid there, so perfect, so solid, so warm.

After a span of time that seems both eons and mere minutes, my father scooped them from neglect and forgetfulness with the long arm of a skid steer. Now they sit—obelisks of memory to the work of men's hands.

13

ANAKY

Mother of Joshua, Daniel, Robin, Judy, Venus, Kitty, and Dilcey. Born about 1775. Died date unknown.

I HAVE a special affinity for any of these folks who lived or worked at Lower Bremo, where I have lived and worked. While I love the people who worked at Upper Bremo and Recess, I adore the people who called this place home as I do. That seems silly, probably, to anyone not from here since the space we're discussing is small in the larger world's eyes—just 3,500 acres. But on this piece of land—Lower Bremo—I can wander freely. I walk and drive these roads—the phrase "like I own the place" comes to mind—but of course, I don't own the place, and neither does my dad. But Lower Bremo is the place I call home. I don't have the same freedom of movement at Upper Bremo or Recess. A phone call will grant me access, and I can walk there anytime I'd like, but still. It's not the same. Lower Bremo is special to me in that way.

I have cried over heartbreak as I walk the trails by the old slave quarter. I have put my face close to the boxwood on the big house's front lawn so that I can get washed over with the smell of home. I have put my hand on my mother's just-cooling face moments after she died. This land—it's filled with my stories.

So when I read that Anaky lived at Lower Bremo, I feel a special pang of wanting to know her. The feeling is akin to homesickness or something like that feeling I get when I meet someone who went to my same college at another time; we share a place, a sense of geography, a knowing that is unusual and rare. The sharing is precious because it ties us together, people of one space.

The first mention I can find of a woman named Anaky (pronounced Annie-ka with a stress on the first *A*) is in the will of Hartwell Cocke, The General's grandfather. A woman named Anaky is left to his son Benjamin, The General's uncle, but Hartwell's wife is given "use" of her until Benjamin comes of age: "I give to my wife the use of Isaac, Annacay, and her child Hannah." The year of this will is 1772, so it's possible that this is the woman I know as Anaky—the years aren't that far off—but if it is, her daughter Hannah does not come to Bremo. This Hannah doesn't appear in the records here at all.

The first sure mention I have of the woman I know named Anaky is on an inventory for The General's Bear Garden Plantation. The General inherited this land from another relative, perhaps his uncle Benjamin, and thus, perhaps this is how Anaky came to be in the central part of Virginia instead of down in the Tidewater, where she originally worked and was owned by the Cocke family. By 1801, The General has sold Bear Garden, and Anaky is now living at the plantation labeled "No 2" on an 1801 inventory. This is the plantation that came to be known as Lower Bremo.

It is likely that Anaky was a field hand since nothing on any of the inventories or other documents indicates she had a special trade and since most of her children are listed as field hands. Aside from knowing that she was a "non-professor" and that she, as the inventory from between 1834 and 1840 oddly says, "lives in doors," I know very little else about her. She had eight children, and her son Daniel married Primus's daughter Dinah. Her daughter Judy had five children, including Armistead, the man Lucy Skipwith married and then left with after emancipation.

Anaky lived a long life, appearing on records as late as 1842. But after that point, I haven't found any mention of her. She doesn't show up on inventories or in any of the letters I've read. We don't have a marked stone that shows her grave or gives us an approximation of the year she died. She simply ceases to appear in the documents that tell us about this time.

It's likely she died of old age. The fact that in 1842 she's listed as between 55 and 100 shows that she was, by then, already too old to work, as 55 was quite old for someone doing hard field labor all of her adult life.

When I think about Anaky, I ponder her name because that is the one solid thing I know about her that is truly hers, not a fact about her children. I wonder where it comes from. Some of the sources I've found suggest it's African, Igbo particularly. This possibility is intriguing because it is one of the very few African connections I've found related to the people here at Bremo. Because the Cocke family had been in the United States (or the colonies as the case would have been) since the early 1600s, they had likely owned slaves for much of that time.

The Cocke family had come from money, so they were not white people who ventured here as indentured servants or even those escaping persecution, at least not in the way we think of Pilgrims. So they would have come with servants, perhaps indentured ones, but almost certainly by the mid-1600s, they would have had slaves. So it is possible—given the way that slaves were passed down as property in wills like the one Hartwell Cocke wrote—that they did not buy many people who would have considered themselves African. Instead, the growth in the number of people they owned would have come through the natural process of reproduction.

So when I find that Anaky's name may be of Igbo origin, it gives me pause. It's rare to find something related to the people who were enslaved at Bremo and see that it might have a connection "back to Africa." Despite widespread belief, the connections to Africa for many people enslaved in the States were slim, much like many of us who are descended from immigrants (my great-grandparents came from Italy) feel very little connection with "the motherland." Not every slave in America was Kunta Kinte, as powerful at Haley's story is. Many were as American as we are today, generations and generations removed from their African ancestry.

Still, that Anaky might have had an African name—that's intriguing because it suggests a closer tie to the African continent than might be expected. It takes her story back further, maybe to the land from which her ancestors came. The source. The farthest point back that most African Americans can take their lineage. It's a clue. A cipher. An arrow.

I wonder if she knew the origins of her name. I wonder if she cared.

14

MOSES

Field hand. Husband of Malvina. Father of Lavinia. Born date unknown. Died date unknown.

"TURNED OUT." That's what it says next to Moses's listing in the inventory of slaves taken on May 26, sometime between 1834 and 1840. "Turned out."

The document also notes that Moses is the son of Sam and Sissy, that he worked at Lower Bremo, and that "once" he professed Christianity. The "once" is written really tiny, squeezed in with what looks like urgency on the inventory.

Malvina was a spinner on the farm, and Lavinia attended the plantation school. In terms of facts, this is the full sum of what I know.

These things and that he was "turned out." The phrase makes me squint and shake my head. I'm puzzled and amazed by it.

I can only speculate on why The General sent Moses away. Maybe he disobeyed plantation law—went off the farm without a pass, drank, smart-mouthed the overseer. If I want Moses's story to fit the vision of slavery that I sometimes let overtake me, a simple vision that everyone involved with establishing and perpetuating the institution was purely evil with no complexity, no goodness in the slave owners, this is what I must believe: that Moses was turned out for something small, like drinking a little on a Saturday night or stealing a dose of medicine to help a neighbor's sickly child. These stories help support my vision, and focus all the sympathy with Moses, the enslaved man.

But it's just as likely that Moses was turned out because he did, indeed, do something wrong. He could have beaten Malvina or their daughter—thus injuring or "damaging" The General's property. Maybe he was stealing other slaves' rations or thieving from the farm and framing other people for his crimes. It's just as possible—all things being equal (which, of course, they were not)—that Moses was turned out because his actions were those that most of us would consider wrong—assault, abuse, rape, murder even.

Sometimes, though, it's difficult for me to make a criminal Moses fit neatly into my image of the ever-innocent slave, given that any crime of his was paltry in comparison to the criminal brutality of slavery. It's hard to elicit sympathy for a criminal, and I want people to see the power dynamic that kept people enslaved, the evil of a system that took away all choice. I'm fearful that if enslaved people are known to not be innocent, then people will write them off as deserving of what they got. I'm fearful of this because it happens.

Yet, I do the people who were slaves here a massive injustice if I do not write about them in their full complexity. By hiding their potential flaws, I deny their humanity, and I risk their dismissal if someone thinks I have been dishonest. No, I must tell the truth: I do not know why Moses was dismissed. It could have been an injustice. It could have been the epitome of justice. I just don't know.

I do know, though, that to be turned out from a plantation was the worst kind of punishment, an exile at best and a death sentence at worst. If a slave left a plantation without a pass—as the phrase "turned out" implies—he was breaking the law. If he was found by slave patrols, it would look as if he was a runaway. The standard practice would be to return him to the plantation he ran from, but in this case, that plantation didn't want him. No one could legally buy him as he was still technically someone else's property. Yet his master refused to have him on the plantation. He was an exile with no rights, no home, and not even the scant protection that the plantation gave him.

So to be "turned out" meant to be homeless and always on the run. A terrible fate.

I can imagine what Moses might have done on the day he left. Hunker down with free blacks in the area. Run north and hope to cross the Mason-Dixon. Live in the woods near the farm so he could see his wife and daughter. But I don't know what he did. No one does.

Malvina, his wife. Maybe she pleads at The General's side in his study, standing there, hands clasped, asking that her husband be forgiven, that The General show the mercy of the Heavenly Father to her husband. She asks, is turned down, and walks away silently. Her only option.

She might have begged because she wanted Moses to stay. She might have begged because she wanted him to leave. Maybe she was battered and, thus, feared what would happen in the privacy of the slave quarter that last night if she did not ask on behalf of her husband. She worked in the house. Maybe she had more influence, more of an ear. Maybe Moses thought she did.

Maybe she didn't ask. Maybe she stayed silent—out of fear of The General, out of respect, out of hope.

On the day Moses left, she may have been at her spinning wheel as The General passed by her. She looked him in the eye for just a moment; then, he walked on.

That night, Malvina sat with Lavinia. They were by their fire, warming their dinner of black-eyed peas with a little fatback. Lavinia told her mother about all that Miss Louisa taught her in school—her letters, all 26 and the numbers up to 12—she got confused after that. A lull. A bright quiet. "Baby, I have to tell you something," Malvina almost whispered.

Lavinia looked up.

"Your daddy, your daddy, he's gone."

She's a quiet child. "Why?" she asked.

"Master has turned him out."

"Oh." She pleated the calico of her skirt over and over again. "Will he be back?"

"No, baby."

Lavinia dropped her head to her mother's shoulder. They sat in silence and watched the peas boil.

There is nothing more to tell. I don't know where Moses went. I don't know if he ever came back. I don't know if he died. If he moved. If he lingered.

There is a Moses on the plantation documents a few years later. Just listed. No family affiliations. No reference to faith or work or housing. It could be him.

It could be that he was let back on the farm. That he repented or feigned it. That The General relented or got tired of complaints about the "turned out" Negro around town. It could be that this is a different Moses, just another man named after the one who turned a stick to a serpent and cursed all of Egypt.

Except this Moses, the one who was turned out, his people were taken in chains out of the African countryside. Their wilderness began in the deep of the ocean, not the deep of the desert. And it didn't end when they reached the land some called Promised.

Whatever the facts of Moses, husband of Malvina, father of Lavinia's life, this is the truth. He lived. Here. On this land—this very farm—where I am writing these words. It is certain that his feet and hands touched soil that I have chewed out of my fingernails. He was a part of this place, as were Malvina and Lavinia and The General and the hundreds of others who have worked and lived here by choice and by compulsion.

Moses's story began here, born to Sam and Sissy. Whether it ended here, I cannot say. But this I know. His story lays claim to this place as much as mine does, as much as The General's does, as much as the life of anyone who has lived here. This is his place no matter why he was turned out of it. It lives in him. And him in it. For better or for worse. Like a marriage, assigned or chosen. Permanent. Unending.

15

MALVINA

Spinner. Wife of Moses. Mother of Lavinia. Born about 1803. Died date unknown.

MALVINA. Her name means "breathing sweetness from her eyes," but I wonder if she did. Was she the girl with round cheeks and a curl tucked under a kerchief that I can see sitting by her spinning wheel? Quiet, subdued, seeing but not participating . . . an observer that everyone assumes is innocuous, almost invisible (as if she, her family, and friends, weren't already supposed to be invisible.)

Her husband had been turned out, after all. Such an experience surely could turn a woman to something other than sweet.

Maybe she was quick-witted and sassy, Ani DiFranco 200 years early. I am most curious about her temperament. I want to believe she spoke nails, but somehow, when I try to really see her, I think she was silent and wise, the observer.

Maybe she wrote down what she saw. Maybe she was the

woman children gathered around, the one whose skirts little ones naturally hid behind. Maybe she sat and rocked them when they cried.

I have this image of Malvina spinning in front of a fireplace, the sandstone floor cold beneath her feet. She is near the dining room, where everyone passes by, and she simply sits and spins . . . her foot tapping the treadle rhythmically, a soft song strung out into the air. I see the wool in balls, the basket beside her made by another woman on the plantation, her friend. She takes up a new ball and twists it into the strand in her hand, making sure it's solidly knotted to the old, and then she picks up her tap and her song again. For hours, all day, spinning until her hands ache, but loving it. There is comfort in the motion.

I wonder if she watched The General's children sneak sweets from the kitchen, the cook's eye seeing but turning away. She witnesses Miss Louisa trying to comfort little Cary when he falls on stones and scrapes his knee, feeling compassion for a woman trying to mother her stepchildren, seeing Lucy Nicholas be the one they chose, watching Louisa's shoulders sag each time. When Berthier and the other men talked quietly in the corners about what they had seen on their trips north, when they talked of freedom and the railroad, she listened, letting her dreams spin out into the thread that would, soon, clothe her with promise

I do not spin, but I often dream of it. Maybe this is where my dreams of Malvina come from. I see myself by a fire spinning out the stories that go on around me, losing myself in the rhythm of the treadle, the whirr of the flywheel lulling out all noise. I want to believe there is comfort and solace and story in spinning.

Her hands held the comfort of all her kin and even those who were not her blood, the people who required that she sit and spin as her labor. Her livelihood depended on it because with Moses "turned out," she knew that The General was not above sending someone away. If Moses hit her—somehow, I cannot get that possibility out of my mind—maybe she came into the house one too many times with a bruise on her cheek, unable to duck her head quickly enough to avoid Miss Louisa's eye, unable to turn away when little Sally wanted to put her hand to the purple and yellow swelling. If so, maybe she didn't miss him. Maybe, instead, the whirr of the wheel filled her up enough.

That wheel of hers—for it must be hers even though she could never take it with her—is full of men and women. The footman who holds the spinning wheel steady on three legs, that long, center post that is mother-of-all, the maidens that carry the pieces that actually spin . . . this is the world of work in a tool. The world she knew well. The women holding it all together while the men bear the weight—for good or ill, as was their due or wasn't. She knew this, the way the world works, even as she knew the way of the wheel. I think she knew and still she stayed quiet. For she had learned that to speak is, perhaps, not to gain.

So now, Malvina, woman of quiet who I wish was a woman of fire, I will try to be her voice, if she will allow me the honor. I will tell those who will hear—those who choose to speak more than to listen but also those quiet ones at the spinning wheels of their lives. I will tell them about her, Malvina, wife of Moses, mother of Lavinia. I will tell that she was strong, that her hands could crush walnuts, but that tenderness was the trueness of her soul, sliding out into the pads of her fingers that crafted the finest wool ever known on this farm.

In 1823, for Christmas, Malvina received a blanket from The General, a blanket she probably spun the thread for herself. This was her Christmas present, her only one; she took it quietly and laid her face on it at night, feeling the wool slide beneath her fingers as she drifted off to sleep. Her strength carried her through years of marriage without a husband and through nights and nights alone.

One day, if I ever have a daughter, I will consider naming her Malvina because of her name's beauty, yes, but also because of her, the woman who watched, who spun out the days in strings. I will name my daughter Malvina because I will want her voice to be hers—a whirr, a steady, solid whisper of strength.

16

HOPEWELL AND NEW HOPE

W hen I arrived in Montgomery, I didn't quite know where to start. For a couple of years, I had worked as a research assistant at the Martin Luther King, Jr. Papers Project at Stanford, and so I knew this city, Dr. King's city. So sacred, so monumental that I wanted to whisper.

I had only a few hours here, and I needed to use it well. The history of this place is separated by a century from my research, and yet, here the legacy of slavery and emancipation played out again. This time the drama unfolded in the city rather than on country plantations. This time TV cameras and reporters captured everything, leaving a record. I could not skip past Montgomery.

I went to the center place—Dexter Avenue Baptist Church. As I pulled up and saw the building so familiar from the many photos that passed across my desk at the King Papers Project, I felt inadequate—I should be doing something holy, special to mark this moment. But it wasn't Sunday; there were no scheduled worship services. And it was too early for a tour . . . and besides, tours never quite do a place justice anyway. Maybe nothing would. So I took a picture and walked over to lay my hand on the brick. I imagined Dr. King's voice low and rumbly in my ears. Just a moment here, on this busy street corner, to pay my tiny tribute of time.

Then, I drove up the street to the Civil Rights Memorial and walked around the fountain where the names of people I had studied were etched beneath the surface of the water—Rosa Parks, John Lewis, Claudette Colvin . . . I took more pictures. I walked back to my car.

Overwhelmed, I left town. I had come to Montgomery as a stopover, the airport city I had chosen as my landing location. I had not prepared to be in this place. I was ready to go further back in time. This seemed too close, too now. Nothing I could do in that city would match up to the history held there; I needed to find these stories I was trying to tell. I needed to build in the backstory for this movement. I headed west, toward Hopewell and New Hope.

From Tuscaloosa, I drove down Interstate 59, my music loud and my optimism high . . . right into a traffic jam. Using my trusty smartphone on the median of an exit, I found that if I simply turned around, crossed the interstate, and headed south on a parallel road, I would be exactly where I thought I needed to be.

Such was the case for the entire week.

A few miles down what must have been the major thruway 40 years back, I made it to the road I needed, a tiny strip of pavement just one and a half lanes wide with no center line. I wove my way past the timbered land that reminded me of the place we'd all come from in Central Virginia. I followed a white van until I was sure he thought I was tailing him; I could almost feel his relief when he turned and I didn't. Eventually, I made my way to Union, a tiny town with the only reference to Hopewell that I could find. Hopewell Cemetery, which sat behind

Hopewell Primitive Baptist Church. The place I had been seeking.

But not the place I was looking for.

At the edge of the graveyard rested a flat white stone, laid over what I assumed was a casket. There was no etching—no name, no date—but the stone was piled high with big, plastic floral arrangements. Clearly, the person buried here was loved, so I wondered why her stone was uncarved: religion, expense, a mixture of both?

As I wandered through the cemetery, calling out for snakes to let me pass, looking for the names I knew—Skipwith, Creasy, Nicholas, Randall—I saw others I knew and remembered: Colvin, the 15-year-old girl who refused, even before Mrs. Parks, to give up her seat on the bus; Crispus Attucks, one of the first men to die in the American Revolution. Stones here had collapsed on themselves, obelisks tumbled from their bases. But the grass was cut, and someone brought these flowers.

These people were not forgotten.

The people I sought, though, were not here.

I KNOW THAT A PLANTATION, in the broadest terms, stands as a cultural marker of oppression. I know this. And yet, when I think about the word *plantation*, I still think "big house." Columns. A long straight drive marked by trees. A building. An edifice.

It's an odd thing to know a plantation existed, to know the events that happened there, to be able to imagine the faces of the people who lived there, and yet not to see the place itself.

When I took this trip to Greene County, Alabama, following the trail of Lucy Skipwith, Champion, Spencer, Kessiah, and the 46 other people who were moved from Bremo to The General's Alabama plantations, I was expecting to find Hopewell and New Hope, the houses or their ruins, with relative ease. I thought it would probably be like the Bremo plantations are here—these massive houses and swaths of land that most people in the area have never seen but have heard rumor of. I thought I'd pull up into a couple of driveways or stop by the local library and someone would say, "Oh yeah, Hopewell . . . that's over . . ." Off I'd go to gaze at standing chimneys or maybe even the whole house, the vacation home of some Birmingham millionaire. But, of course, I had brought Bremo to Alabama with me.

Instead, what I found was, well, nothing. No house. No ruin. No long line of trees that clearly marked a driveway. Nothing.

When I left Hopewell Cemetery, I was looking for someone who might know the area. A man was just getting his mail across from a tiny, brown house with a neatly trimmed yard and a big oak in the front.

I pulled up and asked if he had time for a question. "Yes, ma'am," he said, and searched his brain for someone who might know the answer. He pointed me to a house around the corner. I shook his hand and drove on, realizing only later that his running engine and his mechanic's uniform meant I had stopped him on the way to work. He had helped me without hurry.

The corner house was littered with debris, a children's lifetime poured onto the lawn and mixed with the neglect of a life hard-lived. A boxer barked his squeak-box woof at me from behind a run-down shed. I knocked.

She opened the door, heard my question—"I'm looking for some information about a plantation called Hopewell"—and invited me in. Right into her living room. She cleared a space on her couch, and while I watched a few minutes of Dr. Oz talking about weight loss, she called at least three people to ask them what they knew. I jotted my address and number on the back of an envelope, and she said when her friend got the information about the church, facts, or names I thought might lead me to Hopewell Plantation, they'd mail it or drop it at my hotel. I never did hear from them, but then, that's probably because they didn't have much to tell me.

It quickly became clear to me after an hour or so with local history books in the Eutaw public library that the plantations were in what was now Hale County (formed out of Greene in 1867), so I moved east. Through a series of Internet searches, I found a Cocke family cemetery near the Hale County airport, and I drove around again. I can't quite remember what made me certain that I was in the right spot, but I was certain. Something about the land and the place and the names, it just said these plantations were here.

So I did what I knew to do. I headed down south from where the family cemetery was and started cruising the charcoal gray, two-lane roads, flat and straight enough to make me think Iowa, not Alabama. I wandered down Route 69 from Greensboro and turned west, following signs for the Cattle Ranch. I thought a ranch might be a former plantation, but when I pulled up to the gatehouse and saw the Department of Corrections sign, I turned back around and hit a bigger road pretty quick.

Just up the road a piece, I saw two older, black men standing by what looked to be a makeshift garage. I pulled in and stepped out to talk. They nodded, didn't smile, but turned to face me. "Hi. I'm looking for two old plantations—Hopewell and New Hope. You ever heard of them?"

Both men looked down in the way that showed they were thinking, really thinking, and then they both shook their heads.

"Skipwith, Creasy, Johnson—know any of those names?"

"I know some Johnsons," one of the men said and looked me in the eye.

"I'm trying to find the people related to the folks who were slaves on those places."

A nod from the man who knew Johnsons. The other man began to tinker with the machines nearby. I explained a bit more of what I knew, what I was seeking—of Cockes, and farms, and the cemetery up the road. It didn't help. They just didn't know.

"Do you know any Benisons?" the man still facing me asked.

"I don't, but I'll look for you," I said and wrote his name, his grandfather's name, and his great-grandfather's name in my black notebook. "I'll look and get back to you."

We talked for a few minutes. They tried to help but didn't have much to add. I drove away and waved as I went.

Two days later, I returned to Mr. Benison's house with an envelope full of generations for him. Back seven times into history. He nodded, thanked me, and invited me in for dinner. I declined and drove away.

AT THE SPECIAL Collections Library of the University of Alabama ("Roll Tide Roll"—I think I have to say that out of deference), I introduced myself to the archivist who gladly pointed me toward the handful of boxes in their Cocke collection. I flipped through pages and pages of letters and receipts . . . to find exactly what I was seeking: the list of people sent to Alabama in January of 1840. Perhaps this list was also extant in the Cocke papers at UVA, but finding it there, in just a few boxes hundreds of miles away, somehow that seemed crucial, so important.

I jotted down every name. George . . . I fill in the Skipwith that isn't there. Daniel, Champion, Armistead, Squire, Dinah, Becky, Mima (Miama, as I know her), Kessiah—that blessed girl. I almost cried there in that quiet room where teenage girls looked for the photos of the first years when black sororities were allowed on the campus. I breathed. We were here. We were found.

THE NEXT MORNING, I grabbed breakfast at Flava Restaurant right in Greensboro. Just a little place with Formica tabletops and an open kitchen. Grits, eggs, toast with grape jelly. As I stood to leave, I asked some diners if they knew the people I was seeking. No, never heard of them. But another customer told me to stop by this house with the white tires out in Sawyerville (I'd pass through there on my way down from the hotel), that Mr. Benson might know. Benson, Benison . . . yes, I thought I'd do that.

Flava's owner suggested I try the barber next door, and when he didn't know anything, he suggested the library. So I headed around the corner to find it closed up tight—not open on Thursdays.

I defaulted to the courthouse—not sure why it hadn't been my first stop—and headed into the records room. I was just into my first Will Book when a woman came in and set herself up with the Probate Records across the standing desk from me. Clearly, we were doing similar work; no one scours these massive tomes for simple pleasure. As we chatted through our scanning, I found out she was doing research on her family, people who had been enslaved in Hale County and who were owned by two prominent families in this area. I told her about my research, and we chatted away the morning. Kindred spirits, but sadly, her people were not my people. I wished I could help her. I wished she could help me.

Then, a man came in and took pity on me. He realized I was looking through the indexes of every single Deed Book (I'd exhausted the wills by that time) and that I'd be there until 2050 if he didn't help. He handed me the comprehensive index and then asked me who I was looking for.

Before I knew what was happening, he was making copies of maps for me and showing exactly what tracts of land formed the two plantations I was looking for. He introduced me to a woman in the courthouse who owned one of those tracts of land. He handed me a business card—Nicholas H. Cobbs, Attorney at Law—and asked if I wanted to see the land. Now, this, this was an opportunity I couldn't pass up.

A couple of hours later, he dusted off the seat of his pickup and drove me out to the farm. We had to stop at a catfish hatchery to get the key, and then we hauled our way over there by the airport in his pickup. We opened the gate, drove past the salt lick, and ended up at the Cocke family cemetery. Some of the names were ones I knew—John, Elizabeth—but these were not people with whom I was familiar. They were cousins back then . . . their kin would be so far removed as to almost not seem like blood to the Cockes I know now. I took some pictures, and Mr. Cobbs and I discussed how he might get a crew to fix the tombstones. Then, we closed up the chain-link gate and got back in the truck. I took pictures of the big oak trees—those natural indicators of where big houses might have stood—and we drove back out.

Mr. Cobbs took me up to the top of a hill behind a little brick church and told me an old house used to stand there. The house he thought might have been Hopewell. But it was torn down, long gone.

It seems that plantation houses in Alabama are not the same as those in Virginia. In Alabama, the homes were wooden with wide-swept porches to keep the air cool (so I learned after a little research later). None of the brick grandeur here . . . quieter homes somehow. Perhaps that's why The General did not spend much time here.

So my search took me to the graves of people I didn't know and wasn't that interested in researching, to some old trees that might have marked a house, and to a trailer park where an old house might have once stood. There were a lot of questions in that place.

But then, the questions would have been numerous in the 1840s, when The General sent his people here. When The General first devised his plan to move families to the Deep South where cotton was making the rich richer, he had not yet been to Alabama. Instead, he was going on the word of his cousin John, whose children's graves I saw, and on the words of other wealthy plantation owners who invested in the potential yield of cotton. Whether or not this hope for wealth was The General's central motivator for sending his slaves to Alabama, I cannot know because he layered on a plan for his people to buy their freedom by working the land.

He believed that if there were higher crop yields, his people would be able to buy their freedom sooner, in as few as seven years. Of course, they also had to follow his standards rules for emancipation (and for life on the plantation as well): confession of Christianity, allegiance to temperance, no fighting, no leaving the farm without permission, no guests without passes, and no swearing. If they could follow these rules (without falter) and earn their value—from $1000 to $3000—by working the land, they could be free.

Then they could go to Liberia. There was no hope of staying in Alabama or even returning to Virginia. The cost of freedom was travel to another continent.

So the Skipwiths and the other families that traveled to Alabama in 1840 must have gone with hopes, too. Faint, confusing hopes of freedom and of buying themselves and their families. Fifty people walking from Virginia to Alabama, unsure what they would find, taking all that they owned with them, carrying everything except what they had known and the families they left behind.

It makes the questions of my trip there—via airplane with a small carry-on and a return ticket—seem so small. So minuscule. So easy.

I try to imagine this group with twenty children under 14 walking all this way, chains around their hands, maybe their throats. I wonder what they talked about as they walked. I wonder if they imagined the fields of cotton, saw them as clouds or curses. I wonder if they talked of good times in Virginia or just celebrated the chance to be free, as they were promised.

When these gangs of people walked up to Hopewell house, the one-story building with its metal roof so different than the three and four stories of slate-roofed houses here, they stood, still, silent, for a while. A study of what was to come. A collective sigh, a turn toward their homes now. A promise of hope, perhaps too good to be true.

17

GEORGE SKIPWITH

Overseer at Lower Bremo and Hopewell. Husband of Mary. Father of William, John, James, Lucy, Jenny, Ursa, Critty Ann, and George. Born Christmas Day 1802. Died date unknown.

HE WHIPPED PEOPLE. He whipped people because they didn't work as fast as he thought they should work. This fact makes my heart ache because I want to like George; I want to respect him. But I don't.

I want to see George Skipwith as a victim of the system, not as part of it. But perhaps that's the worst part of chattel slavery—sometimes the victims became the perpetrators.

George was born on Christmas Day 1802 here at Bremo, the son of Jesse Nicholas and Lucy Skipwith. He had eight siblings, including Peyton, who emigrated to Liberia with his family. I imagine he did what all the children here did—played, went to school, worked. I can see him, a little boy with flecks of straw in his hair, climbing the oak tree in front of the Upper Bremo house and hiding there while the carriages full of dinner guests arrive.

Maybe his uncles, the postilions on The General's carriage, wink up at him when they come in at dusk.

Maybe because of his family's good name or because of his strong work ethic or sadly because he was a big man, the only man, in fact, whose size and skin color (very dark) are noted in the records, George grew up to be trusted around the farm. Eventually, The General made him overseer at Upper Bremo, where he managed the work distribution and oversaw the progress of all the operations on the plantation—from work in the fields, to purchases, to the hiring out of his fellow slaves. His position placed him just under The General in the hierarchy, above even Primus as foreman.

It's not clear why The General gave George this position. The General certainly had an esteem for the Skipwiths, and so maybe he hoped to help them, further down the road, to "earning" their freedom with this appointment. Or maybe it was a cost-saving measure—a master does not have to pay an enslaved overseer. But most likely, The General made this choice because he had a hard time—as did many plantation owners—keeping white overseers. With George in the position—a man who had no choice but to stay and do as he was ordered—he could assure himself of some stability.

I don't know how George managed a position of prestige that required him to work his friends and family like animals. A position between two worlds where he needed to seek favor from The General and at least respect from the people. It's not a position I envy.

Maybe for that reason or for others, George began to drink. If such a label existed at the time, the historical record seems to indicate that he was an alcoholic. On a farm where the master was a temperance advocate, having an addiction to alcohol was among the worst offenses someone could perpetrate. Because of his affinity for drink, George was relieved of his position as over-seer after a few years.

What's curious to me is that just a year later, The General put him in charge of operations here, on the farm where I grew up, Lower Bremo. But apparently, this bit of favor did not last either. George and several other slaves were found off the plantation without passes, and it seems George had taken to drink again. He was again relieved of his post.

Yet, still, a few years later, George is put in charge of the group of 50 slaves who were moved to Hopewell in Alabama. For as firm as The General could be about some people—selling Richard off the plantation and ensuring that the new owners would never let him return, turning out Moses without sale or pass—it seems that when it came to George, The General was a bit more tender. Maybe he thought more responsibility would turn George around, reform him, save him.

While most of the time I would be inclined to be glad of The General's soft heart, I cannot find my way to it because from all accounts—even the letters George wrote himself—George was a brutal, abusive overseer. The reports of his use of the whip are far more frequent than accounts by any of The General's other overseers.

Because of George's abusive tactics, his seemingly unmitigated desire for power (a potential problem in any workplace but particularly in chattel slavery, where subservience is necessary for the maintenance of the structure), and his continued drink-ing, The General takes harsh action. After his final attempt at curbing George's problems—George's demotion to foreman and the installment of a new overseer at Hopewell—The General sells two of George's daughters, women he saw as strumpets. The General, in his own words, does this "without remorse."

From where I sit in the 21st century, it seems The General should have been able to predict what would happen—George drops even deeper into drink. It's easy for me to see this, though, knowing what we do now about alcoholism. But then, it must have seemed like a possible way out for The General—the problems on the farm diminish with two women he saw as troublemakers gone, women whose moral laxity he blamed entirely on George, and perhaps George gets the jarring he needs to reform.

In The General's world, where he controlled most everything about his day and the days of his children, this choice must have seemed logical—punish the father by removing the daughters. I can't condone it—I could never condone the sale of human beings—but I can see how he might have thought it would be effective at, if not saving their father, saving his other people from ruin. It was not.

The next year, in 1851, The General decided that George's mere presence was harming the work and morale on the farm, and he sent George, his wife, and young son (also named George) away, to where is unclear.

I don't know quite how to fit George into my concept of chattel slavery on this place. I don't know whether to put the blame on a system that tried to break the will of even the strongest men. Maybe it broke George, and he felt his strength had to come out in other ways. I don't want to excuse George altogether either. He chose to whip people, despite his master's desires that he not do so, at least not so frequently. He must have gained something from that behavior—power when he felt powerless, the fear of the people he oversaw—a fear he might have felt toward his own master. I don't know.

In the 1860s, George, his wife, Mary, and his son George were moved again, this time to live and work on a plantation in Columbus, Mississippi. Sometime later, maybe after emancipation, George, Mary, and young George returned to Alabama, settling in the community called Cedarville with several of the other families who had been enslaved at Hopewell. After this, I can't find what happens to George or his family.

What I find, instead, are the requests for a presidential pardon from George's namesake, Planter George Skipwith, the man from whom I suspect the Skipwith family on Bremo took their name.

Perhaps here, in a crime that requires a pardon—the owning of another human being—we find the root of George's tragic story. Or perhaps the root is located in humanity itself—our desire for power and escape. Perhaps it's some of both, all mixed up in a man who knew the whip from both ends.

18

ISHAM GAULT

Cowherd. Son of Hannah and Dick. Father of Hannah. Born about 1804. Died date unknown.

WHIPPED TWICE IN ONE DAY. George whipped Isham twice in one day. In an 1847 letter to The General, George says

I gave isham too licks over his clothes for covering up cotton with the plow. I put frank, isham, violly, Dinah, jinny, evealine and Charlott to Sweeping cotton going twice in a roe, and at a Reasonable days work they aught to hav plowed seven accers a piece, and they had been at it half of a day, and they had not done more than one accer and a half and I gave them ten licks a peace upon their skins.

Twelve swings of the whip against Isham's body. It's hard for me to imagine any behavior warranting that kind of punishment.

It does seem, if George is representing the situation accurately, that Isham and the other field hands were moving very slowly in the process of "sweeping cotton," or plowing under the stalks of the already-picked plants. Still, the idea that such slow move-ment deserved whipping is abhorrent. But then, this is a different time and a different system. Maybe I just don't understand.

That same day, Isham's sister Julyann was whipped for hiding her hoe, so maybe there was just a run of laziness or extreme fatigue running through the folk on the farm. Or maybe George was just hell-bent that day. It does sound a bit as if it might be the latter from the rest of George's letter from that day. In it, he describes whipping a total of 10 people, including Robert, whom he almost whipped to death. But then John Cocke, The General's cousin and overseer at Hopewell, told George that perhaps the other three people with Robert—who had purportedly given him lip—should have gotten the same treatment. It's hard to know who's wrong here—the people whipping or those being whipped. I do know that whipping is never deserved and that these were people working in a system that gave them no power of protest or complaint.

Yet, still, it seems as if Isham's family kept getting a raw deal, and not just in the stripes left from the whip. His dad, Dick, died when he was very young, maybe still a toddler. His sister Mourning was hired out; living away from her family may have made her name more true than she'd have liked. She had a daughter but she wasn't married, a situation of which The General surely didn't approve and which may have been the reason he hired her off the farm. The General sold Isham's brother-in-law, the man married to his sister Letty. For a time, his twin sisters Miama and Julyann, the girl who was whipped, were hired out. It didn't seem much as if The General wanted the Gaults around.

The Cocke family legend says The General liked to keep families together. But here, he didn't. He sold Letty's husband and then hired out her own daughter.

The only person in Isham's family who seemed to fare well was Joan, his brother Sam's wife. She and Sam lived in the log house, and their two children—Bibyanna and Pompey—were enrolled at the school, the only children in the Gault family to be so. Of all the family members, Joan is the only one listed on the 1830s inventory as being a professor of Christianity. Given that The General would only consider people as possible candidates for emancipation if they professed his faith, it doesn't seem too much a stretch to think he might have also treated those "professors" more kindly than he did others.

Yet, in 1837, The General sent Isham to Hopewell, where he was given the same conditions to obtain his freedom as everyone else. Yet, Isham did not, as was the case for almost every other person there. Instead, Isham lived on in Alabama even past emancipation. In 1870, he is on the census list for Cedarville, living alone but next to a woman named Hannah, who was his daughter, and two of his grandchildren, Julia and Samuel, named after their great-aunt and uncle, perhaps.

Isham is listed as a stock minder, and the census taker recorded that he couldn't read or write. It seems he didn't attend school or, if he did, he lost his literacy from disuse.

When I picture Isham now, I draw on this time in his life—the time when his grandchildren lived next door and his neighbors were old friends from back in Virginia—the Mosses, the Kellors. I see him on his porch, listening to Samuel and Julia laugh and play. She's about seven, Samuel's about two—she's put Samuel in a dress and is trying to get him to sit for tea at a little table under a tree in the yard. There are no teacups, no cookies, no chairs even. Just a tiny round stump that is the table, but they are laughing. Isham is watching them from his rocking chair, easing back and forth. It is 2 p.m., and he is content to not be out in the heat of this August day, with his back bent over cotton fields. He smiles quietly at the sounds of giggles by the old stump. He thinks about walking over to join the party.

Then, Julia says, "I'm gonna whip you, boy," when she's pretending that Samuel spilled his tea. Isham is out of his chair before he even knows his feet are on the ground. He stands over the tiny girl, and as she cowers, his face softens and he says, "Child, we never say we are going to whip anyone. We don't do that to people we love; we don't do that to people we hate. Whipping isn't right. You hear me?"

She nods, and he takes a seat on the ground beside her. "Can I have some tea, please?"

With her tiny hand, she pours from the imaginary teapot into the imaginary teacup Isham holds between three fingers. He takes a tiny sip and proclaims it, "Oh so good." Then he passes Samuel the tray of cookies and says, "You both know you're named after your aunt and uncle. Let me tell you about them."

19

KESSIAH

Cook at Upper Bremo. Wife of Charles. Mother of Cain, Matthew, Frederick, Charles, Cary, Albert, and Abby. Born about 1805. Died date unknown.

KESSIAH, Kiziah, Cissiah, Cessiah, Kizzy, Kissire. Her name changes over and over, with each semiliterate recording in an inventory or in her own letters.

When I add her last name—Morse by Miller's reckoning, Morris in some census lists, Moss if the people I know here in Virginia are her kin—suddenly, this woman could be exponentially more than one person.

She appears on a list of births, kept on the upper half of a sheet of paper that also tallies the birth of puppies, as "Sally's girl Kiziah"—1805. In 1821 and 1823, she receives a blanket, her 1823 "gift" to be carried with her when she is hired out to a man named Edy.

Then, I lose track of her for a few years, probably because she is living away from the farm at Edy's place or maybe at other places around the area. So when I came across her name on the list of people who were moved to Alabama in 1840, one among 50, my heart leapt. There's Kessiah, my friend, I thought.

From there, I learned that she was hired out regularly as a cook in the town of Greensboro. I wondered if I saw some of her genes in the woman who made breakfast for me at that restaurant called Flava, if perhaps the cook used Kessiah's recipe for making grits. This is wishful on my part, a desire for more connection than I can rightly or reasonably expect.

After emancipation, Kessiah and her family stayed in Hale County, near Greensboro, in Cedarville, as did so many of the other people who came from Bremo. Then, as the pattern goes, I lose track of her. She could have changed her surname or moved, or it could be that I'm just not getting the right combination of spellings for her first and last names. Or maybe, simply, she died.

I can't find Kessiah, but her family lived on there in Hale County until 1900. Her granddaughter Abby, Cain and Matilda's daughter, shows on the census there, still living with Cain. In fact, I can find many, many of Kessiah's grandchildren—at least 24 of them —and they carry the names of Bremo with them. Peyton, Chapman, Diana, George, Ann, and even a John Hartwell. Her granddaughter Phillis has the Cocke surname because her father, Cary, who can only be named after The General's son, carried that surname. The names carry the places of their lives down through the bloodlines. I would love to know if there is a Chapman or a John Hartwell Morse/Moss/Morris living today.

Some of the baby-name books I look up online tell me that Kessiah means "polished, refined." That seems fitting for a cook. Others say it means "cinnamon-like bark" also right for someone who spends her days in food. These two meanings don't seem to work together, though. Things that are polished are usually bark-free and smooth. Cinnamon isn't smooth—it adds texture and depth. Perhaps she lived this contradiction.

Another baby-name site tells me that "Kezia \k(e)-zia\ as a girls' name is pronounced ke-ZYE-ah. It is of Hebrew origin, and the meaning of Kezia is 'cassia tree.' Cassia is the generic name for a variety of trees and shrubs, one of which produces cinnamon." In the Bible, Kessiah is one of Job's three beautiful daughters he is given after he has passed God's test. Kessiah, Keren-happuch, and Jemima—Cinnamon, Dark Eyes, and Dove. The promise of the names shows why they were chosen as gifts for new children, and not just for syrup bottles.

The Puritans started using the name Kessiah, and carried it here with their righteousness. It was a name of the fair, the pure. Somewhere that name jumped racial lines and came to this Kessiah, a dark-skinned woman, and she bore it forward, misspelled, probably mispronounced, this woman of refinement and spice.

Kessiah carried this name from dairy to kitchen when her arms were elbow deep in biscuit dough. She carried it to the garden below the big house where she picked peppers and tomatoes for a summer salad. She carried it to the table of the man who could not even spell her name the same way twice. She carried it to her bed where she curled against the side of her full-flung husband and rested to the breaths of the seven bodies that issued from her.

She held her name in the corner of her mind, a treasure, a gift from someone, a blessing laid on her by a woman, for only a woman can know what it is to be both polished and cinnamon— smoothness and grit. Someone gave her this name; she whispered it to Kessiah as she slept. She sang it when she rocked, and it became her breath. Her very essence.

Kessiah carried this name from Virginia to Alabama when her

family moved. She carried it into Hopewell, a place thought to bring a glimmer of light to the tired eyes of her family and friends but that, for many, was just another plantation, just another place to work without freedom.

She carried it off that farm into the homes of the people who hired her to cook for them. She carried it in their back doors and onto their kitchen counters where, still, she put her arms elbow deep in butter, flour, and milk and stirred the white dough into biscuits of air. She carried it home at night where she turned over her wages to a man who claimed that she deserved to be free but never let her be so.

I see Kessiah, woman of refinement, woman of flavor. I see her here in this place where I live. I see her with her jaw set firm and her eyes flinty. I see her carrying on, for this is what she must do, what women must do. She carries her name through 200 years, and I see her. Her head is held high, her neck straight. She is proud. She is Kessiah.

20

LESSONS FROM THE SCHOOL BUS

I t is a credit to my parents that it wasn't until I was long past high school when I realized that I had been one of only three white kids on my high school bus (the other two were my brother and the daughter of the bus driver). I never noticed. This was just our bus, the one that picked us up first and dropped us off last.

Now, I cannot help but wonder if Mrs. C, the bus driver, reversed the route in the afternoons on purpose—so that she and her daughter would not be the only white people there or if her route was simply about convenience to her home. She still drives the same route. Maybe I should ask. I probably won't.

Each day, we left school and took a brief detour down by Burning Bush Baptist before hauling more than 10 miles down the highway to Fork Union. Then, Mrs. C hung a hard left, and we wound our way back to West Bottom, the poorest section of the county. A place the white people of the county did not often go.

We passed yards bare of grass and with barrels for burning trash. Driveways washed out so badly that it would have been impossible to pass over them with a car if the people who lived there had actually owned one. We saw young men gathered in groups on porches and in yards, their hands tucked deep into pockets—jobless, bored. It is the poverty I remember from this place, not the race of the people there.

Our high school was pretty evenly split—black and white—when I went there. But I wouldn't call it integrated. Not really. There wasn't much outward animosity, I guess. There just wasn't much mixing.

Maybe it was this division that kept me from thinking about the history of Bremo and how these people on my bus might be related to it. Maybe it was that no one at Bremo really talked about the slave history beyond the sort of accepted references to geography—the slave graveyard being the only place acknowledged as real. I'm not sure what it was, but it wasn't until college that I started thinking about this history and how much I had been ignorant to it.

But when this realization hit me, when it occurred to me that Anthony—who terrified me because he had a huge head and was, honestly, kind of a bully—or Chiquita—whose friends called her Chi Chi and who was murdered the year after I started driving my brother and me to school—might be connected to Bremo as much as or more than I was. It wasn't until even more years later that I realized that the people I shared a school with might be descendants of the slaves from Bremo.

I wish I had realized that then, 20 years ago, but what would I have done with that realization? I'm not sure there was room to talk about such things. It seems to me that division should open up space for dialogue between people, but it doesn't. It shuts it down.

It turns out that the people from West Bottom were not descendants from the enslaved people at Bremo. The West Bottom folks are probably descended from people at other plantations—Spring Garden, Point of Fork. The Bremo descendants ended up over on Mountain Hill Road, on land adjacent to Bremo still.

I cannot help but wonder what it would have meant for me to know the history of slavery in general, of Bremo slavery in particular. Maybe I would have noticed the racial and economic divide so evident on my bus. Maybe I would have tried to cross it, to talk with people more, to mix it up a bit. Or maybe I wouldn't. There is no room for what ifs in the conversations of history.

But today, almost twenty years after I graduated from Fluvanna County High School, here is what I know: that bus route taught me something—it taught me that the legacy of slavery lives long in our relationships, in our neighborhoods, and in our memories. Even if we can't or won't see it.

21

JAMES SKIPWITH

Waiter, steward, riverboat captain. Husband of Patsey. Father of two children. Born 1825. Died 1860.

JAMES WAS BORN at Bremo to George and Mary. His aunt was Lucy, the schoolteacher, and his uncle was Peyton, perhaps the slave best known here because of his family's central focus in the one published book about these places. *Dear Master* is a collection of letters written by slaves and former slaves in Alabama and Liberia to The General and collected in the 1980s by Randall Miller. Some of Peyton's letters appear in this book.

After living until his young adult years here at Bremo, James was sent to Belmead Plantation, where he worked for The General's son, Phillip St. George. By this time, James was married, and his wife Patsey and children—whose names I have not yet found—were owned by Cary Charles, another of The General's sons. James was sent to Alabama alone in the late 1840s and spent eight years working toward buying his own freedom. Yet he could not buy his wife and children or persuade, even with The General's intervention, Cary Charles to free them. So when on November 12, 1857, he sailed for Liberia as a free man, he sailed alone.

I cannot imagine his grief as he boarded the *M. C. Stevens* out of Norfolk on that late autumn day. It is doubtful that Patsey and the children were allowed to make the several days' journey from Bremo to the coast to watch the departure, so James boarded that ship alone, having left everyone he loved at Bremo . . .

I am so sad for him—for a man who had to choose between freedom and his family. To be free . . . but alone.

I can't imagine what Patsey felt. She could have asked her husband to stay, suggested he forgo this opportunity and remain close by, or she could have encouraged him to go, to live—for all of them—the choices that they did not have. I wonder how she explained James's choice to her children.

Or maybe it wasn't a choice. Maybe The General said that James had to accept manumission—accept his freedom—and leave or be "turned out." Maybe there was something of The General's reputation staked to James's life. Maybe it was a cost-cutting measure. Maybe.

To me, the saddest part of James's situation was that it did not have to be this way. The General did not have to require that the people he "freed" leave the continent. There were free people of color all over the South, some living adjacent to this property here in Bremo—the Cawthorns, the Nestors, even Archibald Creasy, a man who was emancipated by The General but not sent away. Instead, The General's ideas about what America was supposed to be kept him from seeing this possibility, or perhaps he simply thought it best if all black people went back to Africa. I cannot say.

Maybe that's the biggest tragedy of this whole Liberia plan altogether—that people could not see that there was no threat, beyond the one they perpetuated sometimes purposefully, in black people and white people living together.

The General was an active member of the American Colonization Society (ACS), an organization that sought to buy the freedom of enslaved people under the condition that these people would then be sent to Liberia to colonize it for Christ. Their perspective was called gradual emancipationism, and it has been touted by some people over the course of the last 250 years as a reasonable, reasoned approach to the legacy of slavery.

In fact, Marcus Garvey and his Back to Africa movement shared the central tenant the ACS held so dear—that blacks and whites could not get along in the same society. For many people in the ACS, the problem was the "inferiority" of the black race. For others, the central obstacle was the prejudice of whites against blacks. Sending freed slaves "back to Africa" solved the problem from both ends of the spectrum, the ACS argued.

I, even recognizing my 21st-century perspective, cannot get past the massive historical irony present in this act. People from Bremo whose ancestors were stolen from the continent of Africa, although almost certainly not from the region known as Liberia, are sent back to a land they have never known as a condition of their freedom. The hypocrisy and ignorance in The General's practice—in fact, in the actions of the ACS as a whole—amazes me. I am stunned by the level of rationalization involved in justifying and funding a process of returning African Americans to a land they never knew as a requirement for emancipation.

Rather than try to overcome the racism that told them black people were less than capable or unintelligent, rather than recognizing the social constructs that made advancement by black people so difficult, rather than accepting their own culpability and taking responsibility for it, rather than even acknowledging the level of affection they felt toward the people they owned, the ACS sent people to a place they had never seen and could not culturally recognize. This feels tragic to me—to separate rather than to overcome—but then, that's not an unusual choice, I suppose. Just look at our legacy here in the United States.

Yet, even the people The General was freeing, even James himself found hope and wisdom in this plan. "It's the best country in the world for our race," James said in a letter back to The General. I don't know if that's accommodation on James's part, a desire to say what The General wanted to hear. It could be, and yet, there's something in the tone of James's letters (collected in *Dear Master*) that seems to indicate he genuinely comes to this belief as he talks with Liberian leaders and weighs the alternatives "back home."

It's difficult for me to know what to think of James. The idealist wonders how any man could leave his wife and family behind. The realist in me knows that this was his one shot at freedom, and perhaps his one opportunity to obtain freedom for his wife and children. Maybe he thought Liberia would give him a bigger earning potential; maybe he thought he'd be able to bring them over. Maybe I'm being naïve about the nature of his marriage.

What I do know is that James and Patsey never saw each other again.

Almost 8,000 people were sent to Liberia as the fulfillment of their emancipation requirements. Eight thousand people. Men, women, children sent to a place they never knew. They were expected to farm—something most of them knew well—and many of them thrived. But many of them also died, of malaria in particular. I don't know how anyone can call this good.

James Skipwith lasted two years in Liberia. In 1860, five years before his family would be freed by law, he died. Malaria took him. I don't think we can call that freedom at all. Not even a little bit.

MINERVA

Daughter of Tom and Daphne. Sister of Madison and Monroe. Born 1830. Died date unknown.

SHE WAS NAMED for the goddess of wisdom, and her brothers for two of the most prominent men in Virginia at the time of their birth. Their names portend auspicious things for them all. Yet, almost all the knowledge I have of Minerva is included in that bold listing above. I'm not even sure about her date of birth but have extrapolated it here from an inventory taken on June 1, 1840, where she is listed as under 10 years of age, and an 1846 Tithes List, where she is said to be between 12 and 16.

I know that her family lived in the stables at Upper Bremo. I know she and her brother Monroe were in school on the plantation. I know her brother Madison was the oldest because he appears alone on an inventory from 1827. It's not much, but it does tell me that Minerva lived, which is more than most people know about her.

I am fortunate. For many, many people who do this kind of research, there is nothing to go on but a first name or maybe just a gender and an age (for example, "Male, 32"). Occasionally, there's only a gender and a price ("Female, $400"), and sadly, historians of slavery have had to learn to pull a great deal of information from these scant facts. A young man (in his late teens or 20s) was the most valuable slave a person could own because they were the most capable of physical work. Next in line was a young female slave because she could produce male offspring. Of least value were the old people because they could neither reproduce nor work well. So when a researcher knows that the master bought a 22-year-old man, he knows he paid premium price for him. Or if by chance the price is listed and is low, the researcher can determine that perhaps the enslaved man is injured or maimed in some way, less able to work and, thus, worth less.

It's sad when we take the parameters of a system and use them to tell the story of individual people, but sometimes, that's the best we can do.

As I ALWAYS DO WHEN I'm researching these people, I built a family tree for Minerva in Ancestry.com. I entered the few things I know—"Minerva. Born about 1830 in Fork Union, Fluvanna, Virginia, USA. Father—Tom. Mother—Daphne. Brothers— Madison and Monroe." Nothing. The search pulled no listings for a Minerva in this area.

I tried again, this time searching "Minnie." Often people used nicknames on legal documents at the time, perhaps because that was how the person recording put it down—in the diminutive— perhaps because that was the only name they knew for them- selves. Minnie . . .

Minnie Edwards. Barbour, Orange, Virginia. She shows up on the 1880 census with approximately the right birth date and a birthplace of Virginia. She is black. She is a widow. She has eight children—five girls and three boys. Clara, Jarrett, Robert, William, Louisa, Phillip, Alvina, Caroline.

I think this may be "my" Minerva for a few reasons. First, people who used the surname Edwards lived here—Ned, Felicia, Lucy, and Berthier. Secondly, the names of her children speak of this Bremo—Jarrett Spring, where the Temperance Temple originally stood and where a slave quarter was located; Phillip, The General's middle son; and Clara, Phillip's wife. Too many intersections for me to ignore the possibility. So I connect the census record to Minerva's entry and hope something comes of it.

Perhaps I will find that Minerva's last name is not Edwards. Perhaps I will have to remove this connection and move forward in a different direction. But for now, this feels like progress, and it gives me a place to move past the wall a bit.

Because all the documents and research tools I have available have run dry, I turn to the only other source I have—people. I write on Facebook: "Central Virginia Folks, does anyone know members of the Edwards family in Fluvanna or Orange? Specifically, I'm looking for descendants of Minerva (Minnie) Edwards and Berthier Edwards." Within minutes, my friend Bonnie says that a man with the last name Edmonds should be able to help, and she tags him in her comment. I haven't heard from him yet, but I know the Edmonds family; I went to school with Anthony. They're a black family that has been in the county for a long time. In this small place, it's possible that they will know how to help.

We will see. Until then, I'll just revel in the little girl Minerva, 10 years old but carrying the name of a goddess when her brothers were named for mere mortals. I'll imagine her reading her books at school and knowing, when the Cocke children play school with her, not to correct them when they are wrong. I will see her as wise, wiser than the nickname Minnie would suggest. Not a mouse, but a goddess for sure.

23

OLIVER CREASY

Husband of Judy. Father of Mollie, Lucy, Nash, Tucker, Maxwell, Lavinia, Martha Ann, Agnes, Ardelia, Charles, Robert, and Marshall. Son of Anthony and Lavinia Ann. Born 1837. Died date unknown.

A FEW MONTHS AGO, all I could have said about Oliver was that I knew he lived here at Bremo as a child. I had his name on an inventory list and that was all.

Now, I know that he fathered 12 children with his wife Judy. That he was the grandfather of Eugene Creasy, who today lives just over a ways, on Mountain Hill Road. That he is the great-grandfather of my friend Joe Creasy, who treats me to dinner when we meet to talk about this book.

I know that Oliver is descended from three of the most prominent families here—the Creasys, the Skipwiths, and the Nicholases. His paternal grandfather, Ben Creasy, was the carpenter here, and his maternal grandfather, Jesse Nicholas, the shoemaker. His maternal grandmother was Lucy Nicholas, the nurse to the owner's children. I only wish I knew what his paternal grandmother, Judy, did here. Okay. I wish more than that—I wish to know Oliver and his family as people. But that is an impossible wish.

Oliver's uncles traveled the world. His uncle George moved to Alabama, where he was overseer on the owner's plantations there for a bit, and his uncle Peyton was given his freedom and then passage to Liberia, where he helped found the new country at the behest of the ACS.

I know Oliver's people. Yet, I still don't know Oliver. He is, perhaps, the linchpin of this story—the person who draws all the themes of this book together, and yet, even the most important slave is, by history's comparison, not very important at all as a person. Not to most people.

What I wouldn't give to have just one story about Oliver, one tale about him as a kid climbing one of the massive white oaks and then having to call his father, Anthony, to get him down as the sun set on the plantation or about how he carved amazing animals out of scavenged wood. Maybe Oliver was the man who hid the owner's horses in a quarry during the Civil War, the one Bremo slave who made it into a newspaper article, albeit not until the 1920s. Maybe. All I have is maybe.

I know that Oliver lived in Scottsville, just up the James River, in 1870. I know that Judy was still living then and that several of his children—Mollie, Lucy, Nash, William, Maxwell, and Lavinia —had already been born by that point. I know that Anthony and Lavinia Ann lived next door. On this census, Oliver, Judy, and all their children are listed as mulatto, a designation that could mean that Oliver had both white and black ancestors or could simply mean that the census taker thought him fair enough to have white blood, as erroneous as that kind of indicator can be. Nothing in the records clarifies this designation.

Ten years later, in 1880, Oliver and Judy are back in Fork Union, the district where Bremo is located, with Nash, Tucker, Maxwell, Martha Ann, Agnes, Charles, Robert, and a now-married Mollie (Bates is her new surname). Here, Oliver is listed as mulatto but Judy and all the children are "black." The malleability of these definitions less than two decades after emancipation both follows the laws set forth in slavery and prophesies the way that attributions of skin color and racial identity would linger long over our country.

This is where my knowledge of Oliver ends: a reference on one slave inventory where he is listed as "under 10 years of age" and a slew of census records that tell me about his people but so very little about him.

Perhaps as time passes, as I read more documents, as people continue to seek out their ancestors, as we continue to value the stories of the nearly forgotten people, I will learn more about Oliver.

Until then, though, this is all there is. Oliver Creasy—born 1837. Died—date unknown.

24

TIME TRAVEL

Here is both a place and a time.

I know this land; I've known it for over 20 years and yet, when I try to imagine here as it was then, I feel lost. I don't know how to precede my memories—sledding with my brother on this hill, watermelon on the front lawn, Mom in her living room chair—and see what was here. I jog these roads; I walk these trails. I wander across fields and gaze over the vista, and yet there is so much I don't see. So many footsteps and carriage rides and Model As and infant births. So many crop rotations and wagons loaded. So many weddings. So many deaths. So much time.

Sometimes, I sit on the lawn of this plantation and look over the hills, past the railroad tracks, where I have squished many a penny, to the low grounds and the wall of trees that blocks the James River from view, and I try to imagine what I would have seen on this same day at this same time in 1863.

I picture it like those movie flashbacks where everything goes wavy. Out of the fields come the silhouettes of people working. Behind me, I hear the faint rattle of pans as the cook makes lunch for the man who owns this place. I look down to see my legs now covered in a skirt, long and heavy with hoops and crinoline.

The railroad tracks are gone, replaced with the towpath for a canal. I sit there long enough to see the slaves who are hoeing the fields stop for their brief lunch—take bread and pieces of chicken out of the fabric packs they have tucked by the edge of the field, out of the sun. I watch three people—one man and two women—sit down together on the grassy hillocks to the left of the great red barn.

I hitch up my heavy skirts and make my way down to them. Their faces turn toward me as I walk closer; their brows furrow before turning placid again. I slow as I realize that no white woman from their time would do this. I resolve and walk on, asking if I can join them. The man nods slowly. I curl my skirts around my legs and sit down on the grass.

"I'm Andi," I say and stretch out my hand. My arm hangs there. I am so eager to hear their names I probably cry—as I am now—149 years later, even imagining these introductions.

I want to break all the fictional rules of time travel and tell them when I am from. I want to tell them that these farms will still be owned by The General's family in 149 years. I want to tell them —cautiously—to just hold on. That in two years they will be free, that the Emancipation Proclamation they may think is useless at best, only rumor at worst, will soon make them free.

The man says, "I'm Robin," and takes my still-extended hand. "This here is Judy. That's Louisa." I shake the hands of the two women as they shoot glances to one another from the corners of their eyes. We sit quietly for a few minutes until I cannot hold back another second.

"Are you married? Have kids?" I say.

"My two are Violet and Milly," Judy says quietly.

"Elias and Richard are my boys," says Louisa.

I gasp. I know Elias. Or at least I know his name. I have a copy of the document that hired him out to George Seay in 1852.

But I realize that for all I know, I know nothing. I don't know these people's favorite colors or the funny stories they swap on Sunday afternoons as they sit under trees, out of the sun's heat. I don't know who they love or who they hate or even how they feel about this place or their master. I know only what I might know about a valuable object, the provenance and care. I know nothing of them as people.

Yet, I want to know, and still, even in my own vision, I cannot.

I would like to tell them that this place is still a plantation, but people are not owned here anymore. I would like to tell them about how this place is worked now, how my dad is the new version of an overseer, but he doesn't carry a whip. I would like to tell them that many of the people who work here are from Mexico, a place that these three individuals have probably never heard of except in reference to war.

I would like to explain so much, including that I am writing a book about them. But to explain the book, I would have to explain that they have been forgotten by the people who live on this plantation and that they are unknown to most others, even their own kin. I would have to tell them they are merely mentioned in history as names, names I have come to love, names held by people I still don't know.

I know they will not understand, these three people in a field in 1863, these who are people yet are now forgotten. I do not understand.

"I'm glad to meet you," I say. I ask about the crops and yields, looking at the potatoes partially hilled. About who is hired out where and when will she come home, "Before Christmas?" They answer politely but do not share more than is required by submissive politeness.

Then, too soon, their break is over. They stand, and I say, "Bye." They nod and move back toward their hoes as I walk back up the hill to the big house; it won't do for me to keep them from their work.

As I come up to the crest of the driveway, I see a white man in a suit leave to get in his carriage. He has a black man with him, and the black man's head hangs tight against his chest. I know this is Richard and almost double over at the sight of him. Richard has just been sold to Mr. Norvell on the condition that Richard can never, ever return to this place again. I know The General is so strong in this stipulation that he makes Mr. Norvell sign a document that says Richard cannot even be allowed to trade on the canal that runs beside where his mother works with her back to him now. I know The General will go even further and require that Mr. Norvell demand the same things of anyone to whom he might sell Richard. I know because I have read this document, have a copy in my office just over the hill.

I cry quietly and look down at Louisa bent over her hoe again. She does not even see her son leave for the last time. I watch—as if I can see for her—when the carriage pulls away up and around the bend, just below where my brother's basketball hoop stands.

Then, I return to the lawn; I am broken. I know so much and understand so little. I know this feeling so, so well. I sit and watch for as long as this world stays in this time.

Without the slightest jarring, I come back here to my blue jeans and my loose hair that blows with the same breeze off the James.

Tears are still fresh on my cheeks. I do not wipe them away. Instead, I walk past the big house, through the gardens my father plans so that the beds are brilliant in color at the family gathering on the Fourth of July. Past the oak tree that stands now as it did then. I pass the blackberry bushes planted for my mother and return to my computer, to the only tool I have to travel in time.

I sit down at exactly noon, and I imagine—sitting on a lawn, looking out over a field and hearing those names.

Violet. Elias. Robin. Judy. Richard.

25

CHAMPION

First foreman at Lower Bremo. Born date unknown. Died about 1827.

HIS NAME IS EVERYWHERE in the letters from the overseers to The General. "Champion is also planting his field laying near the shop and has got his new ground nearly logged and above half cultured," says a letter from Upper Bremo overseer Dudley Ragland to The General on April 27, 1807. He comes up again and again in Ragland's letters, and also in those of Moss, another overseer, perhaps at Recess. His work was clearly important enough to report on.

He also seems to have held some standing in the overall hierarchy of plantation management. In 1844, long after he has disappeared from the inventories—a sign that he has probably died—they still call a structure "Champion's House." Throughout the overseers' letters, fields are referred to with the possessive—"Champion's." He's the only person, besides

Primus, I've seen given prestige enough to be considered as possessing—however informally—some piece of property.

I'm presuming this means he was the foreman, but nothing I've found so far actually designates him as such. It could be that I'm just wishful here. Maybe I want badly to know something more of him.

I do know that in 1808 Champion got sick with "pains in his limbs and body which induces one to suppose that it is the rheumatic pains," said Sam Pettit, another overseer. At that time, many things were called rheumatism, just as most lung conditions were called pleurisy. So there's no way to know whether Champion actually had rheumatic arthritis, but if he did, I can't imagine how he managed to work the fields with that much pain and stiffness. His fatigue must have been overwhelming.

In fact, he says as much via Moss when the overseer writes to The General. "Champion informs you his wheat is very likely [sic] and that he will begin to plant corn." He is still sick, however, and says he is "not capable of doing more than attending to his people and see how they go on." Champion worked in a system that valued a person by his ability to work and also to produce a certain amount of product, whether corn, wheat, or tobacco. For Champion to not work for a few days but also feel compelled to tell his master of his illness, he must have been very ill. In reporting his illness, he marked himself as less than.

At some point, around 1808, Champion becomes "Old Champion" in the records. This new nomenclature may have been a result of his illness—perhaps his sickness aged him or simply called attention to his age. More likely, he became "Old Champion" when a "new" Champion entered the farm. I expect this new Champion was Champion Morse, a baby born to Harry Morse and Ann "Sucky" Faulcon. This young Champion was probably named after Old Champion, another sign of the respect folks at Bremo showed to the older man.

I know much more about young Champion. He grew up at Bremo, but then in 1840, he was among the group of 50 slaves who moved to Hopewell. There, he eventually became foreman for several years after Shadrach died in 1855. Eventually, due to poor health—possibly another inheritance from his namesake— he shared those duties with his nephew Cain until 1865. In 1866, he stayed on at Hopewell as hired labor, under Mr. Powell, the man running the plantation, but then, late that year, led a group of former slaves to begin their own cultivation of land in Alabama. Young Champion was married three times and had two children by his second wife. According to the census, he was farming near Cedarville in Hale County, Alabama, in 1870.

Yet, of Old Champion's personal life, I know so little. I don't know if he was married or had any children. I don't know who his parents were or where he was born. I don't even know on which plantation—Upper, Lower, Recess—he lived at Bremo. Like most of the people who were enslaved on these plantations, Champion is a name that is only associated with his work, with the products he brought to harvest, with the land he cleared.

Yet, for me, he is also an ancestor of sorts. He is the man who first did the work to make my home, the man who chopped down the trees for the Chapel Field that I love to watch from my dad's living room in the early morning. He is the man who helped clear the roadways down which I drive or hike. He is the man who preceded my father by effort and time. In so many ways, Champion built my home.

For this, I owe him more than I can say.

26

DILCEY

Nurse. Daughter of Anaky. Born about 1810. Died date unknown.

THE LIFE of this woman is still—after almost two years of research—so very unclear to me. Every time I think I pin down another small fragment of her life, there's a piece of paper that throws that idea into question. For example, on the inventory from 1827, there are two young women named Dilcey, one the child of Anaky, the other the daughter of Billy and Maria. These families lived next to each other in the brick house. I'm left wondering if there were two women named Dilcey, or if someone made a mistake when taking the inventory and wrote down "Dilcey" when they meant "Lissy."

My best analysis—and the intuition I've had to rely on through the process of writing this book—tells me that Dilcey is the daughter of Anaky and that Billy and Maria's daughter is named Lissy. On an 1827 inventory, Lissy is listed as sister to Malvina, the woman married to Moses, who was "turned out." It also seems that Lissy died tragically, "burnt to death," the 1830s inventory says. I have a hard time imagining how someone burns to death. House fire. Kitchen fire. Tragedy no matter how.

So if Lissy has died by the mid-1830s, I am deducing that the woman named Dilcey for whom I have records in the years that follow is Anaky's Dilcey and that perhaps the person who took the inventory miswrote or misheard Billy and Maria when they spoke. Lissy and Dilcey aren't that far apart phonetically, I suppose. So it seems Dilcey is Anaky's daughter, and Lissy Billy and Maria's.

I think.

Probably.

Dilcey's not listed on the 1830s inventory with Anaky's children. Maybe she was hired out. Maybe she, too had died. None of this research is solid. No one has handed me a footnoted family tree that says, "These people are kin to these people." No one cared enough about these people then to record much about them, and even if they had, the shifts of historical time make it difficult to chisel out "fact" based on the fluttery paper and stories of history.

I do know three things for sure about this woman named Dilcey. First, she was hired out to Thomas Childress in 1826 for the sum of five dollars. Boyd Coyner's study suggests that Dilcey was a nurse. Like Lucy Nicholas, she cared for children. It is likely that she wasn't much more than a child herself, a teenage girl probably. She was sent away for a year at a time, allowed to come home only at Christmas (like Nelson at UVA). Not only was she away from home, she was solely responsible for tending and rearing the children in her care while also managing to be deferential to the children's parents, her masters for the time being.

In exchange for this responsibility, she was given a set of clothes and perhaps a pair of shoes. She got none of the money The General earned from her work.

But she must have been adequate at the work because in 1828 she is hired out again, this time to a man named Mayo who lived in Columbia, about 15 miles away from Bremo. She had not even been there two months when she ran away, claiming that she was treated badly. According to Mayo, she had run off with a man "who gathers toll of the boats on the Willises River, associating with the boatmen." To The General, this report would have been very disturbing. He did not think highly of watermen, an opinion that many plantation owners shared. It was watermen who carried word of uprisings and who helped slaves escape their owners.

In one famous case in Eastern Virginia, a group of slaves stole a canoe, paddled across the Potomac, commandeered a ferryboat, returned back across the river, loaded up their family and friends, and made their way to a British gunship sitting just off the coast, where they all found freedom. With stories like these in the mix, it's not surprising that The General had no kindness for the men who worked the canal that ran through his plantation or for any other waterman at all.

After 1828, all records of Dilcey end. It is possible she was found and returned to Bremo. But I like to dream that she and her waterman escaped. The ads about them reached the papers with descriptions—"Negro woman with very short hair and medium complexion. A birth mark on her right arm."—and still no one found them. Maybe they made their way up to the Chesapeake Bay and then on to Baltimore. Maybe they took the trail of Frederick Douglass and moved up through the tip of Delaware into Pennsylvania, stopping at the Underground Railroad's safe houses on the way. Watching for lanterns and listening for whistles as they ran under cover of night. It sounds romantic. I hope it's more.

In 1866, I find the record of another Dilcey, an older Dilcey, maybe an aunt. It is this older woman's story that gives me hope for the runaway Dilcey. The true promise of romance.

27

STONE WALLS

Low stone walls line the landscape here, cobbled together from pasture stones and the seams of rock in the land. They stand about 3 feet high and run hundreds of yards along the edges of fields and through the stands of trees. Sometimes, they mark the line of a roadbed, the edge of property. They etch the landscape, reminding many visitors of the walls that carve the hills of New England and Great Britain.

Now I use these walls as guides to the paths that have been carved by years of foot and cart travel. I stroll Grandmother's Walk, named after The General's great-granddaughter and the grandmother of the previous owners, and find my way by following the stone wall that holds up the roadbed beneath my feet and leaf litter. I see the disintegrating stone wall around the slave graveyard and anticipate the Saturday when Ben Creasy's descendants, Joe Creasy's family, will come and help us build it back to mark the sacred place with stone again.

For me, these walls are sacred, too, built by enslaved hands in the dead of winter when crops were not yet sown and people "needed" to be kept busy. I want to put my cheek against the stones and hear them whisper to me—"Elias put me here." But the stones do not whisper.

THE WALL. The people who research African American genealogy come up against the wall in their work, where the path of information goes cold, where the lineage of these people trails back into slavery.

As I work, I slam into the other side of that wall. I move through genealogies forward in time, toward 1865, reading inventories and letters that mention Cato's work hoeing in corn or Betsy's receipt of a blanket. Then, when I reach emancipation, my trail crashing into that wall, the gap I can't really cross through either.

It is so frustrating, to be standing two feet from the names you need, the people you want to know, so close I could touch them if I could just reach over that invisible but very real boundary that enslaved people know so well.

It's almost as if I can see Dilcey or Ned right there, across one of the slate walls at Bremo. Almost as if I could touch their sleeves if I reached out.

But when I do, my hand passes through them like so much mist.

ELWOOD CUMBO. I type my dad's name into the computer. My grandparents' names pop up immediately. Then, their parents, and their parents, and their parents. In two hours at my desk with a cup of hot tea at hand, I have traced my grandfather's line back to a man named Emmanuel Cambow, an "Angolan" slave who was freed and then bought 50 acres of land in James City County, Virginia, in 1651. I'm descended from a man who was once enslaved, and I love knowing that part of my history. It gives me a lineage that connects back to the very founding of our country, and it ties me to all the other Cumbos—African American, Native American, and white—in the U.S. This fact gives me a story that is as rich and culturally complex as most here in our nation.

Yet, because my family has identified as "white" for most of our time here in the U.S., it wasn't hard to travel back 10 or 12 generations, just a click of a button. I wish it was always this easy.

A few weeks later, I try the same thing with my grandmother's family. I'm lying on her guest-room bed, and I start searching—Bela Brown, Mae Dell Sutton . . . and back I go, three generations, six, twelve, all the way to Anne Sutton, who sailed here from England in 1634 on a ship called the *Hercules*. She was hanged for murdering her own daughter. Again, fascinating information that I treasure as part of my story, part of my legacy. A horror, for sure, and still mine somehow. A story that grounds me to this place, to a people, that helps me know who I am.

I will return to that story sometime, but now, I cannot help but compare my journey to these stories with the journeys taken by African Americans as they seek to find their ancestors. I wonder what it would mean for Joe Creasy to know the name of his first ancestor brought here, to be able to identify the ship and, thus, the place from which his people were stolen. It wouldn't change who he is, just as knowing my story doesn't change who I am, but it does fill in some gaps, like the backstory in a novel. These details may not show, but still, they are there and give foundation to what comes after.

Because enslaved people were not typically allowed to read and write, they often did not record their own stories. Because as enslaved people, they did not legally have surnames and because their owners did not think of them as equals and, therefore, did not record them by first and last name, because Jim Crow enforced separation and oppressed black people fiscally, socially, and educationally, these stories were passed down orally, if at all. If someone forgot to tell a story or found it hard to talk about the decades of enslavement, if a granddaughter didn't tell her children, and a great-grandson his, these stories disappeared. Almost nothing survives if it is not repeated or recorded.

There is no signpost to show the way back through these stories, no click of a button while lying on a grandmother's bed that will carry us back through emancipation and bridge the gap that is the wall.

ON THE STRAIGHT, easy-to-follow lines of a piece of college-ruled notebook paper, I have written:

Letter—J. P. Tucker to The General—Jeffrey died after falling off a horse when drunk. Died Feb 8, 1800, near William Omohundro's place.

That's everything I know about Jeffrey. No surname. No death date. No family. Just that he was sent as a young teen to work a day's ride away in Charlottesville, that he came home for Christmas, and that he was still alive in 1840. I know more about William Omohundro's family than about Jeffrey's. My mom played piano for Omohundro's four-times great-granddaughter Courtney years ago. I know where the Omohundro homestead is; I used to pick up sticks as a church fund-raiser there in the fall. But of Jeffrey, I can fit all I know in one sentence.

Jeffrey's story is typical in its spareness. An example of almost entire elision. As I research each of these people, I put together a time line for them—I think of it as my guiding wall, the one I walk beside as I do this research, the one that my path, almost inevitably, turns me toward eventually.

Some people have longer walls, more detailed time lines. Ben

Creasy's fills two full pages. Primus Randall's and Jesse Nicholas's a page each. Their stories I can fill in more with fact and less with conjecture. But still, most of this work is just picking out the trail of what was once a path, once a life lined entirely by the walls—physical and legal—of the plantation.

I try to quarry the time lines of these stories with various tools. I use online databases for genealogical information, and sometimes a tiny green leaf appears in the corner of a beige box, the software's indication that it has found some record for me to consider—an ivy to decorate this line. I follow the ivy back and see census lists and tax inventories. Sometimes I find names and dates. Sometimes I find entire trees covered in these ivy leaves, the stories quarried and laid out by other people doing the same work.

I take some hope there and sketch out family trees for each person about whom I know more than just a first name—Primus Randall, Ben Creasy, Jesse Nicholas, Lucy Skipwith, Berthier Edwards. Sometimes the lines I cut lead me to another line that I've already followed, a path that crosses another. When this happens, I get giddy. All fluttery in the stomach. As if I've found a new stone wall to follow through the forest, a guide to get me somewhere I haven't been, to tell me a new story.

Sometimes the trail leads me to rooms full of crumbling documents, to hours spent lifting massive books, which can only be called tomes, down to desks in county courthouses. I pore over the pages and decipher the slant of 19th-century handwriting hoping for names I know—Malvina or Aggy, Sucky, Kessiah, George—hoping for groups of names to show me these are "my people," not other enslaved souls on another plantation. I lift book after book until my arms ache, and I know that I have not worked even a fraction of the pain that laying that stone wall would require. I remind myself that I do this work from choice. I press on. Sometimes I find a trail, a roadbed of names, and I track it to a date and a story of a trip to Philadelphia or a horrible death that may be a murder. Sometimes I find a story in all these pages. Rarely. But sometimes.

Mostly, though, I click on these ivy leaves, turn these pages, and trail myself right to the wall, where I am stopped, unable to move further, deeper, into the record. I can wind the ivy all around itself and never get over that short stone wall most days.

On those days, I close my folders and shut down the tabs. And I walk the ground, up the gravel drive to the cemetery, the one place I know holds truth.

A SIMPLE SEARCH. I type "Hopewell plantation Alabama" into the little oval on the right-hand side of my computer screen as I prepare for a research trip there. I'm expecting to find a photo of the house or some historical-society pamphlet. Instead, what I find stops my heart a second.

Mattie Malone, the great-granddaughter of Lucy Skipwith, the enslaved woman who ran the school here and then at Hopewell in Alabama.

The slate wall crumbles before my eyes. I lose my breath. I feel tears push my lids. I have found someone. Someone.

I search for Mattie Malone and read that she died in 2009. I am three years too late. I start to cry.

I return to the newspaper article that brought me Mattie's name and see she has a daughter Carol, a granddaughter Samira. I see where they live. I can call. I will call.

"Ms. Malone?"

"Yes, this is Carol."

"My name is Andi, and I live at Bremo," I hear her breath catch. "Where Lucy Skipwith was born."

We have knocked a hole in the wall; a few stones have fallen away. I have no idea where this path will take me. But I will follow it, as I always do. There are stories here among these stones.

28

LUCY SKIPWITH

**Teacher. Wife of Armistead for a time. Mother of Betsey and
Maria. Born about 1820. Died date unknown.**

SHE WAS SO IMPORTANT, Lucy Skipwith was. The star pupil of
Louisa Cocke when Lucy lived here at Bremo. Of course, this
isn't surprising—her parents were smart people, too: her dad,
George, as the foreman at Lower Bremo, my dad's predecessor in
a sense; her mom, Mary, as the milkmaid at Upper Bremo, in the
dairy I point out on each and every tour that comes through this
place. Lucy was set up to excel.

Lucy managed two schools: the Sabbath school here at Bremo,
and the infant school at The General's Hopewell Plantation in
Alabama. Contrary to popular belief, it was quite legal for The
General to educate his slaves, as long as he did not hire someone
to do so. The first teacher was Louisa, who trained Lucy. But just
because it was legal does not mean it was popular. It seems fairly
clear from the records that The General was beaten nearly to
death in the nearby town of Fork Union for this choice. Even still

he continued in this aim. Lucy—at risk herself—taught school for many years.

Lucy was married to a hard man—Armistead—or so she describes him when she leaves him in December 1865 and writes to ask her master's forgiveness for this choice. A choice she took the first chance she could. Once she was free from one man's hand, she chose to walk away from another. She says in her letter to The General:

I was sorry that I had to part from Armistead but I have lived a life of trouble with him; and a white man has ever had to judge between us, and so turned loose from under a master, I know that I could not live with him in no peace, therefore I left him for I wish to live a life of peace and die a death of both joy and peace and if you have any hard feelings against me on the subject, I hope that you will forgive me for Jesus sake.

I have such respect for her in this decision, even though I cannot know Armistead's side of things. She did what she thought best, and she walked away. A brave act for a woman, particularly a woman of color, in December 1865.

Lucy's strength shines in her love for her daughters, too. When Smith Powell, the overseer at Hopewell, offers to buy Lucy's daughter Maria, Lucy combines her strength with words and her influence over The General to convince him to stop the sale. When her daughter Betsey has been having sex with a white man and The General wants to send her away, Lucy convinces him that she, the girl's mother, can best bring her to hand. When I picture Lucy, I see her with hands on hips, her voice quiet but stern, a woman who knew the system and how to work it.

Both of her daughters had relationships with white men. I use the term "relationship" deliberately here. It is clear from the records that both Maria and Betsey had ongoing affairs with white men. Of course, in this time and in this place, rural

Alabama in the 1860s, such relationships were verboten, illegal, dangerous if they were between a white man and a black woman he did not own. Other standards were in place for masters and their slaves.

It's hard to know whether Maria and Betsey were consenting in these relationships—the account as told by Randall Miller in *Dear Master* seems to suggest they were—and that certainly is a possibility. It's demeaning to say that a black woman could not be in a consensual relationship with a white man, and yet, it is clear that even if they were consenting in any way, their society was not.

Lucy must have been terrified for her daughters—terrified of what the men themselves might do, terrified of what The General could do, terrified of what other whites in the area might do, terrified for what her biracial grandchildren might experience. Yet, she did not let her fear overwhelm her; she used her words, her influence, her power to protect them. A good mother. A strong woman, without a doubt.

Lucy, like her father, George, lived in a space between. A slave certainly, but one to whom The General entrusted much and expected much. A person in authority over other slaves and yet still very much confined by the institution and beliefs of her master. It would be easy to read her as a person who capitulated, who gave in, but the way she—and this is the only word— manipulated The General to protect her daughters belies the idea that she was meek, passive, or deluded. The only word that fits to describe Lucy is shrewd.

Lucy's strength and cleverness passed through her bloodline, playing out in the lives of her female descendants like Mattie Malone. Mattie moved from Birmingham, Alabama, to Cleveland, Ohio, in 1941, another family following the path of the Great Migration. Mattie and her husband were among the first black families to integrate the Shaker Heights neighborhood in

Cleveland. At that time, integrating anything was at best uncomfortable and isolating, and at worst outright dangerous and violent. Then Mattie sidled right up to her legacy and started teaching public school. I wish I had known her.

Mattie's daughter Carol—the woman whose joyful, teary voice called me to Lucy's story like a beacon—has also been an educator and entrepreneur. Carol hasn't caved to the weight of painful relationships and the struggles of life as a single woman. In fact, she has raised Lucy's six-times great-granddaughter Samira to be wise and smart and confident. No doubt Lucy would be proud.

When I think of Lucy now, I see her as a young woman, thick braids lying against her back, a light blue dress hanging just a little short on her calf. I see her with Samira's face, full of hope. I watch for her on the road when I leave the farm, see her looking back at me over her shoulder as she begins the long trek by wagon to Alabama. She waves to me and nods, a small smile on her face.

29

LUCY'S SCHOOLROOM

The schoolroom is still here. The seats are bleachers, black and steep, rising almost a story into the room. Two hundred years later, they are still sturdy enough to sit on, and yet, every time someone does, I flinch. They are sacred, and that is fragile.

The room reminds me of that Thomas Eakins painting where the medical students look down on the surgery in the amphitheater. The oils show the students eager to learn as their master teachers dissect a body for their education. It's gruesome. It's beautiful. It's real.

The students' slates, black also, lie still chalky by the front of the room. I imagine some chemical could pull the chalk shadows from those tiles, and I could see what little Elias scribbled on the dark stone. But I won't do that. These tablets, too, are sacred.

In this space, slave children learned to read and write, calculate basic numbers, identify animals—I can almost hear 15 tinny voices "roar" when Louisa queries, "What does a lion say?" It is a beautiful sight.

Yet, I have trouble seeing the beauty. This is a failing on my part,

I realize. I am so determined to show the harshness of slavery—the cruelty of owning other people—that I tend to want to downplay the gorgeous things. The impulse is fair, I think, for as people we often use the beautiful parts to excuse the horrible ones. But the impulse is not honest—the impulse is selfish. I want to make my work in this telling easier, more simple. That is not fair. Simple, here, is a lie.

So I must admit the beauty—children with raised hands, owners invested in the betterment of people, hope instilled.

Tiny children sat for hours in this schoolroom and listened to Louisa speak—"*A* is for apple." "Eleven is two ones, see?" She stands at the front of the room, her broad skirt and puff sleeves contrasting with the rough muslin shifts and the short, stiff pants of the boys on the bleachers. The children grin in delight at the pleasure of seeing her and getting attention themselves, a rare treat in a place where their parents work all day, six days a week. When a child knows an answer, he bounces with eagerness, fingers rigid with anticipation, arms straighter than the furrows in the fields across the canal.

These little ones really are very little, the youngest of the children on the plantation—perhaps ages four to ten. Too small to work in the fields, children aged for preschool and on up to fifth grade, if grades had existed then.

One of Louisa's star pupils was young Lucy Skipwith, whom Louisa praised often for her quickness of learning and softness of spirit. After all, classroom management was as important then as it is now, and Lucy's pliant demeanor made her a model student. So model, in fact, that eventually she took the mistress's place as teacher and assumed the role when her family was moved to Alabama in the 1830s.

Over and over in her letters to The General from Alabama, where education became her purpose in her master's and, it seems, her own eyes, Lucy speaks of how the children learn well, especially the ones who come every day. She is often impressed by their ability to read and write, particularly passages from the Bible. I imagine her in the evenings bent over a rough farm table with a pile of slates at her elbow. The candlelight captures the curl in a corner of her mouth when Ned spells all his vocabulary words correctly. When Pompey incorrectly adds his two-digit numbers, the creases in her forehead deepen. When she has finished her grading, she takes out paper, pen, and ink and writes to The General about their progress. Like every good teacher I know, Lucy sees her work as more than a job; it's a calling, a vocation, a life's work.

Lucy goes beyond what The General asks of her and starts a night school "for the instruction of the children who work out on the farm." This schooling goes well; these students have a particular aptitude for arithmetic, Lucy notes, and I wonder if that is because they are asked to count their labor throughout the day— so many rows, so many bushels. But when the summer months extend the workdays with the daylight, Lucy writes, "I do not get on with my night school so well at present. The nights are so short, and the children are so sleepy when they come from work that I cannot keep their eyes open no time . . ."

It's easy for me to understand Lucy's distress; she is the teacher, and her students' success defines her own. Yet, the prosperity of the farm takes precedence over education, and this breaks a teacher's heart a little. A good teacher knows that these children's very freedom depends on their ability to read and write. That they are kept away from school by work they cannot choose must be devastating and frustrating beyond any measure I can imagine.

Lucy's disappointment and frustration come through clearly in her letters to The General. What isn't as clear is who frustrates her—the children, the overseer who orders them to work, or The

General who makes such demands on his workforce and his land. She says that some of the students don't come every day, but she doesn't say why. She's a wise woman: she notes that their absence is hindering their progress at school but doesn't place blame. Thus, she avoids calling out her master or his hired man for hypocrisy or poor management while still absolving herself of the responsibility for their lack of progress.

Or perhaps Lucy is frustrated, not by the students or The General, but by her own inability to get these students to learn despite the circumstances. There is something in her tone that makes me think this is so, at least to a certain extent. Lucy's sense of duty is profound—I can hear it in the sadness that spreads over her words when she writes about students not mastering reading yet. I can feel her giving up hope.

As the years pass, her letters become more focused on what is happening generally on the plantation—illnesses, the way the overseers manage the places, her own sewing—and less on her work as a teacher. She shifts from a teacher reporting on her students and becomes The General's witness, a role some might term "spy." Some of this change comes because The General needs someone he can trust to report to him when his overseers are failing, and this trust speaks highly of Lucy's role on the farm. But it also must have been sad for her when her master wanted to know more about crops than about her students' abilities to read the book of Psalms. I'd probably give up some hope, too.

Or maybe she never quit hoping but instead kept that hope quiet and close . . . maybe that was just the nature of hope under slavery.

As I walk into the schoolroom here and look carefully at the benches where Lucy and her classmates sat, as I stand where Louisa and then Lucy stood, I can't help but think of how the beauty of this educational legacy carried forward. The 1870 census shows that many people near Greensboro, Alabama, could read and write, and I can't help but know that Lucy had a role to play in that. In 21st-century Cleveland, of course, Lucy's descendants are still teachers.

Yet, in other subtler, perhaps harmful, ways the legacy continues, too. What people often know about The General was that he educated his slaves. He did. That is fact. A Fact that will not be changed. But that fact is not enough to wash away the other legacy of bondage here. The beauty of imagining tiny children learning their letters and numbers does not overcome the fact that their education, even his own desire to emancipate his slaves once they were educated, was not a priority that outranked The General's own monetary gains; his actions call into question the sincerity of that hope on his part.

For me, this beautiful memory of children roaring like lions cannot erase the image of children working like animals. I wonder if Lucy felt the same way.

30

DESCENDANTS

They came by caravan. Joe's spotless red Caddy in the lead, with an equally pristine black pickup, and a couple of sedans behind. I met them at the barn and led the way up to the slave cemetery. I'm not sure Joe has ever parked that Cadillac in a grass field before, but he sported up and did it without a word of complaint.

As we stood in that field, Joe introduced Dad and me to the line of men assembled—Joe's brothers and nephews and one great-nephew. I didn't catch all their names—too many people for me to pin names on so quickly. But I could see ages—or at least what I thought were their ages. I had thought Joe in his late 50s until a few weeks before, when he told me he was 70, so the men I thought were my age might have been in their 50s.

Joe asked me to tell them all about the graveyard. I tried to find a balance in my voice between tour guide and friend, loud enough to be heard but not authoritative. It seemed wrong to be authoritative about something that belonged far more to these men than to me.

I said that this cemetery was the burial place for some of the people who had been enslaved here. That most of the graves are unmarked, but that we have three marked stones, one for Joe's three-times great-grandfather Ben and one for Jesse, another of Joe's great-grandfathers. We walked through the walls and headed for Ben's grave as I gestured at the line of unmarked stones near the top of the cemetery—"They may have been whitewashed at some point, or maybe they've always been blank." We made our way through crunchy leaves to Ben's grave, and I took a few steps back. This moment and place called for quiet breath and more space.

"Can you take our picture?" one of the nephews asked. They all lined up behind Ben's stone, and I snapped the shot. It may have been my happiest moment of research on this book, to see those men there with their great-grandfather Ben.

A few minutes more of quiet, and the men were eager to do what they had come to do—set the graveyard right. Rebuild walls, reset stones, restore Ben's resting place. So Dad got them started, picking up limbs, cleaning up a tree that had fallen against one wall, setting stones into place to mark corners.

One of Joe's great-nephews, who was seven, and I took to picking up sticks; well, I picked up sticks. He picked up some and then played with the dog—it seemed fair.

I have to admit I had conflicted feelings about these men working here. I so wanted to honor their desire to restore their family's resting place. More than almost any other people, they had a deep emotional tie and a historical rootedness here. So in this sense, I was thrilled to be able to open this opportunity for them.

But part of me was also very sad that they had to do this work. I wish it hadn't been necessary. I wish the graveyard had been kept up and maintained by the owners—the people who owned this property still, the descendants of The General. Somehow, it seemed wrong to see the descendants of enslaved people doing exactly the same work their ancestors had done. I wanted there to be a way for the people who had owned their ancestors to take on this responsibility as part of owning their legacy.

I knew that was not going to happen. Not that the current owners stood in the way—far from it. They were happy to have Joe and his family there but were not inclined to do the work themselves. It wasn't malice or even apathy that kept them from it. This place and the people buried there simply didn't rank high on the priority list of these busy folks. This made me sad and, if I'm honest, a little angry.

Yet, there was something right about Joe's family restoring this place, a taste of redemption, of legacy chosen.

The day went wonderfully. The guys were able to restore one full corner of the original slate fence and set in place massive stone pillars to mark the original gate. They hefted stone and shared all the wisdom of their experience and education to "help" each other get it right. At a certain moment, six men stood around a hole for the pillar and debated for maybe 10 minutes exactly how to repair a stone, each with his own theory of what was best.

There was a quiet moment when I felt my shoulders tense. Joe's grandnephew said, "Dad, we're working like slaves."

His dad put down the shovel, looked him levelly in the eyes, and said quietly, without a waver in his voice, "No, son. We're not. We have a choice."

Then, he picked up a rock and put it in place.

～

AFTER LUNCH, we all climbed on the back of the wagon, and Dad drove the tractor on a tour of the plantation. We started at Lower Bremo and talked about the hunting lodge and the gardens. The men were impressed by chimneys and slate work; as builders and engineers themselves, they articulated their enthusiasm in jargon and numbers that whizzed past my comprehension.

We visited the slave school at Upper Bremo, and they breathed deep. They studied the documents laid on the bleachers, pulling framed piece of paper after framed piece of paper out of the boxes, and Joe's young great-nephew proved himself the consummate kid when he much preferred the exercise bike to any of the history his older family members wanted him to see.

Our visit to the millpond had the men leaning over the dam at precarious angles while they studied how it was put together and talked about the size of the fish they could catch in that mostly untouched water. I shared what I knew—that there were snapping turtles the size of my torso. To me, that was caution; to them, it seemed incentive.

As we left the millpond, we snapped a tie-rod on an axle, and it banged loose as we came back up the hill. Most of the men jumped off the wagon and fashioned a fix from some spare wire hanging from the back of the tractor.

We got home, parked the wagon, and began talking about when they would come back. They had work to finish, they said.

After they left, I began to think about how these men's love of good workmanship is echoed in the buildings around this place. The way the slate roofs have stood, almost untouched, for more than 200 years. How the masonry on the Upper Bremo barn is intact and only slightly bowed after 200 years of weather.

I thought that Ben or Jesse or Anthony or Oliver, Joe's enslaved ancestors, might have done exactly the same thing when an axle broke on one of the carts they were using to haul corn.

I thought, *Ah, but yes, there is a difference*—"We have a choice."
And that is more than a world of difference. More than a world.

31

GRAVESTONES

So tactile. I think if she could, Abra would lick the tombstones. My friend Lynn, an expert on historic African American cemeteries, has recommended we not touch the stones in an effort to keep their deterioration as slow as possible, and I know she's right. But it seems not only useless but wrong somehow to continue to say the kids shouldn't touch. They learn through touch, as we all do when something reaches in or we reach out and scrape ourselves against it.

The Smuckers have come through town on their first week of 12 on the road. The big blue bus—their traveling home—is parked at the Lower Bremo barn, and we are in the slave graveyard. We have spent part of the morning talking about slavery. The oldest two kids—Cade and Lucy—have been to Gettysburg, and they know so much already. About the reasons for war, and civil rights, and owning people. The littles—Abra and Sam—are not so aware, but they are three and two, so maybe they know more than all of us.

All seven of us kneel by Primus's stone, and I tell them about him, the foreman, the father, the grandfather, the four-times great-grandfather. In the photo Shawn snaps, we are all leaning in, tugged as if by Primus's story to his resting place.

These are the moments I live for.

Cade is taking a metal piece of rebar and jabbing it into the ground over and over again, calling to me every few minutes, "Ms. Andi, I think I found something." I come over and dig with my fingers . . . a rock, only a rock, not a fallen tombstone. Cade goes back to stabbing the earth. The kids and I are trying to find more grave markers. It's a task they take to with vigor, even if their child arms aren't quite strong enough to push very far into the soil.

When we all tire—after I am finally able to tell Cade that I think he found something, and we mark what might be another row of head or footstones—Maile climbs into the front seat of the car with me, and her two oldest squeeze the Chesapeake Bay retriever between them as we drive to Upper Bremo, to the Cocke family graveyard, while the little ones go with Shawn for a nap.

We walk through the stone gates and I see Maile note that the wall is fallen here, too. It's not just the enslaved dead who get neglected. I walk with them over to the flat stone farthest from the entrance. "This is Lucy's grave." Young Lucy bows low and looks for the inscription that isn't there. This Lucy, Lucy Skipwith's unintentional namesake who has never known of her until today, seeks to read her name.

While we read and talk, the retriever finds water, and so when it comes time for us to leave, Lucy and Cade get a bit damper and smellier on the ride home. They laugh the whole way.

SHE IS BARELY FOUR, all curls and bows, Miss Makayla, whom I have just met. Her grandfather Bill has driven down with his daughter, son-in-law, and two granddaughters to visit this place where his ancestors—the Skipwiths—were enslaved. Makayla stands now in the graveyard, her outstretched hand tracing the letters—"B-E-N. Ben," she says.

Two hundred years ago, she may have never learned to read those letters. It takes me a minute to catch my breath when she does now. "C-R-E-A-S-Y."

"Creasy," I say. She nods.

As her grandfather, mother, father, and sister come over with my dad, I tell them about Ben. I tell them about Joe, his four-times great-grandson, who is helping to restore this cemetery. I don't need to tell them about Carol, their cousin, who has introduced us all the way from Ohio. I keep talking as we cross to Jesse Nicholas's grave.

We all bend closer to this stone angled far into the ground. This is Bill's four-times great-grandfather. I want to tell Bill all about him. I want to pull out pictures and relay anecdotes, talk about how the other people on the farm respected him and how he had the longest fingers anyone has ever seen. Yet, I have already told him everything I know.

HOLLY COMES IN FROM ARIZONA, the scent of desert air flowing with her. She, Dad, and I sit on his deck and talk. She asks what I think of Dudley Ragland, her four-times great-uncle, one of the first overseers at Bremo. "Was he kind, do you think?" I tell her I have read nothing of him whipping anyone and I know he brought in doctors when people were sick. That tells me he was at least benevolent. She nods. "Considering." I nod back.

We tour the plantations, and she asks if Dudley might have

touched this. When I say, "Maybe," she touches her hand to the pillar, the grass, the wall, her breath following after her skin.

When we reach the definite ruin of a slave house on Lower Bremo, a standing, stone chimney, Holly walks—miniskirt and flip-flops at ease—into the edge of the woods and stands, hands outstretched in what I sense to be prayer and peace. She kneels, places plants, rock, and water from the desert there as offering, and comes back to me. "They are fine," she says. "They want you to look after their grandchildren." I breathe out solidly, relief that I never expected pouring down like water in the desert.

WHEN CAROL and her daughter Samira come down from Ohio to visit, we will start at Lucy Skipwith's grave. Maybe they will bring flowers. Maybe they will cry—my phone conversations lead me to believe that, like me, Carol is a crier. We will drive to the slave cemetery, and we will walk and talk in hushed tones among the bodies there. We will tour these properties, the massive houses, and the quiet, houseless chimneys that are hidden away under ivy and neglect. We will do what we always do when people come to visit . . . but these visits are different.

When the descendants of the people who were enslaved here come, I feel an extra weightedness to these tours. I want to be responsible for their family stories; I want to tell them true. I want to be respectful and honest toward the stories and to these people. I never know quite what to do, how much to talk, and how much to stay silent. I have no idea how this must feel—to find where your people lived, to find some pieces of your story that you didn't even know were there and that you may not have ever hoped to find.

But in a way, these tours are easier because these are people who are here for the real, full history. For the stories of the slaves, not just the home and garden tour of so many historical places. These people don't care so much that The General died in that bedroom there in Lower Bremo. Instead, they want to know how long the slaves worked (from dawn to dusk every day, six days a week except Christmas and Sundays) or where they lived and how far that was from the places they worked. They want the story of this place in its entirety, and the balance of this place's entirety has more to do with black people than with white ones. So when these people come, I feel relief—as if I can now say what I've been parceling to palatable tidbits for most.

When my friends Josh, Trista, and I rode out through the low grounds to the river, I said, "Now, when I come here, I can't help but imagine the backs of people bent low with hoes."

"I feel sick to my stomach," Josh said. I felt like crying.

These stories, they bend us low. They remind us of that from which we came and that the stories from which we come are not always pretty or easy, but they are ours.

"B-E-N," Makayla says. And now she knows his name.

32

ME, NOW

I've become one of those obnoxious people who can't just "let it go." When I walk around this place now, I don't really see what everyone else sees—beautiful homes, gorgeous landscapes, a pristine farm set off from the world. What I see is bricks handmade and carried up ladders onto scaffolding in buckets or hauled on platforms using thick ropes and the ropy, muscled arms of hardworking men. I barely see massive stone pillars set into the ground as gateposts; I see men whose backs are nearly broken with the weight of setting that stone in place. I don't see a spinning wheel as a reminder of practices forgotten but pure; I see women set in front of those wheels, spinning as fast as they can so that they can make enough thread to clothe not only their master's family but their own, too. I just don't see this place the same way I did when I was that teenage girl throwing a Halloween party in the slave graveyard.

I am both saddened and proud of this fact.

Some days, though, when the sun is angled low across the trees and the shadows are long enough to look like drapes, when the wind is quiet enough to make it feel as if the trees are whispering, I see it again—the absolute and profound gorgeousness that is this place. Then I cry.

I STARTED out writing this book to provide a "voice to the voiceless," to be the voice speaking for enslaved people, to be a reminder of what we have, often, intentionally forgotten in our history. Part of me still hopes that this book will be that. But I have also realized how arrogant I was to think I could speak for anyone else, to think I could give voice to an experience that was not mine. I do not know how Lucy Nicholas felt as she nursed The General's children. I do not know how Richard felt as he was sold off of this place so permanently. I do not know how Bill felt when he arrived here to see his family's cemetery. These are not my experiences.

My experience is of a white woman who has realized her own naïveté and ignorance. Writing this book has taught me so much about what I do not know. Even with more than 18 months of research poured into these pages, I still have hundreds of boxes of documents at UVA alone to consider. I still have hundreds of people to study. I still have books and books about slavery and its legacy to read. I have so much left to learn, and even if I read and study it all, I still will have more to know. Yet, this writing has changed me.

Here, above all else, is what I have learned. I have learned that America's decision to use skin color as the method for determining who is free and who is not has wounded us so deeply that—as a country and as individuals—we have to take radical steps to heal this wound. Somewhere along the way—and it will take much more study by me and many others to try and find out where—slavery became not about economics (as horrible as that is) but about power, about one group of people deciding that they could and should control the fate of another group of people. Slavery became about race—about black people's perceived inability to care for themselves or participate fully in American society.

It was this belief that drove The General's ideas of colonization. It was this idea that—along with economic self-interest and self-ishness—drove the Southern states to secede. It was this idea that led to civil war, to massive bloodshed, to a rift in our country that still exists, even as we consider it charming and sentimental.

It was this belief that led to the development of Jim Crow and this belief that drove segregation and the KKK and church bombings and lynchings. It is this belief that we see in our prison systems today and in the achievement gap in our schools. This belief that shows through in our earning charts and in our census data. This belief that keeps black people ghettoized in our inner cities and ostracized in our suburbs. This belief that here in my town in 2012 has black people sitting on one side of the room and white people on the other at a public dance.

If this book has changed one thing about me, it's this—I see this wound, and I am determined to do what I can to heal it.

For me, this has meant ripping back the covering of "history" and "race" that we lay over our prejudices. It has meant staring hard at the way I have been taught, have absorbed, and have even thought my way to racist beliefs. It has meant admitting these beliefs—I once subconsciously confessed to a class that I thought black people lived in substandard housing; I had no idea I thought that—and learning how to change them. For me, this learning has meant I have to do some hard, hard looking at myself so that I can see where I need to change.

For too long, I have remained objective about slavery, laying it back on the shelves of history like some fine linen that I study but never want to tease apart for its stains. I am no longer content to simply study history—I must look for a way to heal its legacy.

Getting to know Primus and Malvina and Gruff and Kessiah and Jesse has taught me that slavery was not just an institution—not just "the way things were done." It was about people—people whose choices to live as they wished were taken away in the most violent, systematic way. Getting to know Berthier and Leander and Minerva and Lucy has taught me that today our issues around race are not just about people—they are systemic and deeply ingrained in how we think of ourselves as Americans.

I have learned my most valuable lesson—that our American Dream of getting ahead through our rugged individualism doesn't work at all when we take away the ability for someone to travel as they please, marry whom they wish, and call themselves by name, when we deprive them of the ability to learn and to earn and to speak. I have learned that America has some dark, shadowy nightmares in our dreams, ones that haunt me even in my waking.

I have learned that I am part of this system, and I am determined to change me. One word, one box of records, one conversation, one story at a time.

33

CATO

Stonemason. Husband of Dilcey. Born 1781. Died after 1866.

WHEN I ASKED the Cocke descendant who currently owns Lower Bremo what he knew about the slaves who had lived and worked here, he said he didn't know much but had heard of a man named Cato, a stonemason.

I don't know why Cato was the only name he knew, but I know that Cato's name is the one—second only to Primus—that has been with me the longest. The name that has been passed down the most.

I'm not sure how these things become memory. Even more, I'm not sure how they become forgotten.

But Cato, his name and his occupation have lingered.

I don't know whether to be happy or sad about this.

Cato was born in about 1781. In 1791, he is listed on the inventory for The General's Buckingham County plantation, Bear

Garden. The General sold this property shortly after the inventory was taken, moving all his slaves across the river to the Bremo properties.

Cato was trusted enough to receive payments for The General, much as the postilions Billy and Phil were trusted, so The General's copious receipts and ledgers show.

In June of 1807, Cato is listed as "ditching" in a letter to The General from Dudley Ragland, the overseer and Holly's four-times great-uncle. The next month, Ragland reports that Cato got his foot badly cut by a scythe.

On December 20 of that same year, Cato asked permission from Ragland to visit his wife on a nearby plantation. Ragland wrote to The General and said, "I am petitioned by Cato to make a visit to see his wife and to start with I am but not knowing your wish upon the subject and fearing Sam might indulge him in riding your colts thought it best not to him go." Five days before Christmas, Cato is refused the opportunity to visit his Dilcey.

I know in 1820 he received a blanket.

In 1826, Ragland mentions that Cato is "willing to stay on and help plant and secure the crop of wheat." I'm not sure where Cato is staying on from. Did he come from Lower Bremo, or from Surry County where The General still spent time? Was he hired out from another plantation?

In 1834, he is listed as working at "UB" (Upper Bremo), as a professor of Christian faith, as a stonemason (with the words "New Canton" in parentheses), and as his "wife not here."

Then, in 1854, the Virginia State secretary of war bought or hired both Cato (marked as "Carter" on this document) and Beck. I don't have any idea why. The Missouri Compromise was signed that year, so maybe they were sent west to fight or work.

By 1866, though, Cato was back in Fluvanna County.

I know this because in 1866, just months after the Emancipation Proclamation, Cato (this time listed as Cator) married his wife Dilcey (listed as Dilly)—the woman who was "not here" in 1834 —legally in the courthouse in Palmyra.

This is one of those finds that made me cry, standing there over the Marriage Book in the Clerk of Court's Office. Tears rolled down my cheeks.

When I found the single-lined note about their marriage, I looked at a man doing research next to me—a man I had never seen and whose name I never learned—and said, "Look, see, Cato and Dilcey got married. They were 85 and 80 years old. They had lived their whole lives enslaved, and what do they do as soon as they can? They make their marriage legal."

"That's nice," the man said and walked away. He had no idea what I was talking about, and besides, crying isn't really the norm in the Clerk of Court's Office. I had to resist the urge to chase after him and tell him the whole story.

The actual marriage certificate is missing, a revelation that nearly caused me to topple from the highest rung of a high ladder where I was flipping through files full of records. All I can find is the reference to the marriage in the 1866 index. "Cator" aged 85 and "Dilly" aged 80. I don't know who they listed as their parents or where they said they were born. I don't know who married them or who was a witness to the ceremony. All those little clues gone, lost to clumsy record keeping or fire or flood. The rest of this story disappeared.

That same year, Cato and Dilcey show up again as Cator and Dilly Cocke on the register of colored people in Virginia. Already in this first year, we have started writing down black people in a separate list, laying the framework for Jim Crow.

After this one additional listing, I don't know any more about

Cato or Dilcey. I don't know if they kept the name Cocke—they could have and just not had any children, or any children who used that name. Or they could have changed it when more time passed and they'd had more moments to consider severing that connection to their former owners. What I do know is that there are no black Cockes here in Fluvanna now.

Of course, they could have also moved away, to the North or another part of Virginia. They could have been fair skinned and thus passed as white for a few decades, until their story became a white story. They could have intermarried with whites and become culturally identified with white people. The Jim Crow South could have made any of these options more desirable than being black here in Virginia.

This may very well be a dead end, where the path of these long lives stops for me. After over 80 years in slavery, maybe they were fine to disappear, to not be inventoried anymore, even for the census. To not have someone write down when they were given a blanket or had a child, to not have that information noted on the same pages with the number of horses and cows born that year. I can't really fault them for wanting to be invisible.

But somehow, I find it poetic that their story ends, for me, for now, with a wedding. There's no party, no witnesses. No double ceremony. No cake, no dancing. Just the quiet record on one line of a book that almost no one ever even picks up. Cator Cocke and Dilly Cocke—1866.

In my mind, though, I see them there at the courthouse The General designed, that Cato helped build—Dilcey in a white dress, Cato in a black suit. They stand there, at the judge's bench, a bench I have touched with tender hands, and they say, in the quiet voices of lifetime submission, "I do" and "I do." They walk out, soft and silent still. Home. Legal, with no one to refuse them permission to go and come. No one to say that their love, their fidelity of at least 40 years, is not fact.

Cato and Dilcey got married. What a beautiful thing.

34

BERTHIER EDWARDS

Plowman. Son of Ned and Felicia. Born 1827. Died date unknown.

In 1866, just months after he was freed, Berthier came back to the plantation and bought a teapot for just over two dollars. I am fascinated by this.

Berthier Edwards was born into slavery. His master purchased him, his sister, Lucy, and his mother, Felicia, from another plantation so that they could be with Ned, Berthier's father. Berthier returns to the plantation where he was enslaved and buys a teapot. Just the idea of that, the specificity of it, makes my heart sing a little.

I envision Berthier on the lawn of Upper Bremo. A man just about my age, 39 years old. He probably walked back onto the farm that day, maybe up the road we now call Teepee Town Road for the Native Americans who lived there—but not in teepees—for a few years. Or maybe he came up Creasytown Road, walking back from Shores, maybe even by the house where I'm told a man named Berthier lived until recently. Maybe his people settled over there with Ben Creasy's family. Maybe.

He walks in for the sale of the belongings that were his master's. Another sale of the type so common on these plantations that were too big to sustain themselves, even with slavery sometimes. The General's furniture is spread on the lawn, his carriages (all except the one I used to see as a teen between the slats on the old barn walls) strung along the drive, his tools leaned against the barn walls. Berthier passes all these things and walks in the front door. For the first time, perhaps.

He strolls through the main hall into the garden room and back to the bedrooms. And walks down the stairs, past the small rooms where his father, The General's body servant, used to sit and press clothes; he enters the library. The shelves of books sit untouched and unread as he passes. It seems impossible to me that he cannot read them, as the son of a house servant on a plantation where there was an active school, but the census takers in 1870 say that he and his sister cannot read and write.

After his tour of the house, after he has breathed in that air that now tastes different—fills him up more—he steps back outside, this time through the breezeway toward the kitchen, and comes back up past the "hotel" where his father lived before his mother, he, and his sister were bought back. He stands at the edge of the crowd by the white oak that holds a swing today. He waits.

Standing there, hat in hand, the August sun bakes against his suit, the one purchased just for this day. The shadows of oak leaves fall against his shoes shiny with newness and polish. He doesn't speak to anyone.

They auction off the big things first—highboys and sideboards, the carriages, the tables. They place huge sets of books on a table by the front pillars and pound the gavel as each set is claimed for a price Berthier can't imagine paying for something that has no practical purpose. He waits.

Then, the kitchen implements come—sets of china, glassware, silver. Many enslaved people and newly freed people invested a great deal of money in what we now academically call "material culture." Even the poorest among us like to have nice things and display them. But that is not Berthier's way. He's not buying to show off.

The teapot comes up to the block. If The General has succumbed to the fashion of the times, he owns a ceramic Chinese-inspired teapot. Berthier bids just twice—$2.00, $2.20. He wins.

I don't know if he came to buy that specific thing that day or if he just saw it and envisioned his father's hands wrapped around its bent handle and pouring from it slowly in his memory, filling the dainty cup on The General's side table. Maybe a vision like this spurred the purchase. Or maybe he just saw the teapot, knew he could probably afford it, and decided to bid. And if he was going to bid, he was going to win. There was a principle at stake here.

Two dollars and twenty cents to help pay the debt of the man who kept you and didn't sell you. The man who kept you and didn't free you.

What I do feel fairly certain about is this: Berthier came to the auction that day deliberately to get something. If not an item in the auction, maybe something more esoteric. The chance to do as he wished in this place. The opportunity to bid, as anyone else did, on something. The chance to walk off this land free.

Berthier wraps the teapot in an old cloth under his arm, pays the auctioneer with his coins, and then turns to descend the front-porch steps. He pauses to look back at the house, hears them start to auction the tools—the plows, the hoes, the rakes—and his pace quickens. No need to see any of those things anymore.

He walks off the land. No pass. No permission. Just two feet in new shoes walking away because they want to.

In 1870, Berthier still lived in Fork Union, in this town, so near where he was enslaved. The teapot rests on the table he made for himself from trees he felled on the end of his small parcel of land. The teapot sits alone and waiting.

ACKNOWLEDGMENTS

Many thanks to the Cocke family, who believed in this project and supported it thoroughly.

Thanks, also, to my dad. You gave me a year, Daddy, and thus, you gave me my footing.

Thanks to the people of Greene County, Alabama, and Fluvanna County, Virginia, for sharing their stories, their homes, and their wisdom.

To Jennifer, who not only edits with the best of them but fills my days with just the right amount of snark.

My deep thanks to Philip, for believing, for every minute, in me and my words. I love you.

Most of all, my deep thanks to the descendants of the Creasy, Skipwith, Malone, York, Ragland, and Nicholas families. To look you in the eyes and say, "Here, this is your grandfather," was my highest honor.

ALSO BY ANDI CUMBO-FLOYD

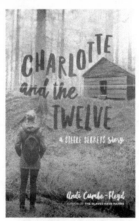

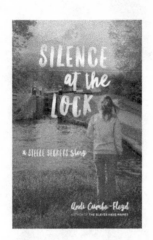

BLACK HISTORY AND GENEALOGY UPDATES

If you're interested in getting twice-a-month updates from Andi about her work on African American genealogy and history as well as reviews of great books in those areas, please join her mailing list.

Join here—Andilit.com/ourfolkstales

NOTES

7. A Place's History

1. More about his agricultural practices can be found in Boyd Coyner's dissertation, *John Hartwell Cocke of Bremo: Agriculture and Slavery in the Ante-Bellum South*, published in 1961.

ABOUT THE AUTHOR

Andi Cumbo-Floyd is a writer, editor, and farmer who lives at the edge of the Blue Ridge Mountains in Virginia with her husband, son, four dogs, three cats, six goats, and plus/minus 40 chickens. Her other books include the Steele Secrets series and *Love Letters to Writers*. She writes regularly at Andilit.com.